KARLOLOGY

Karl Pilkington

Karlology

What I've learnt so far

KARL PILKINGTON

Dorling Kindersley

LONDON, NEW YORK,
MELBOURNE, MUNICH, AND DELHI

First published in Great Britain in 2008 by
Dorling Kindersley Limited,
80 Strand, London WC2R 0RL

4 6 8 10 9 7 5
KD127 – 08/08

A CIP catalogue record for this book
is available from the British Library

ISBN 978-1-40533-746-5

Jacket photography by Ben Morris
Model photography by Guy Archard with additional photography by Sarah Ashun
The publisher would also like to thank the following for kind permission to use
their images (a-above; b-below/bottom; c-centre; f-far; l-left; r-right; t-top)
Corbis: 94–95; Francis G. Mayer 70bl; The Gallery Collection 186–187; Getty
Images: GK Hart / Vikki Hart 140–141; Arthur Sasse / AFP 19clb (Einstein), 169bl
(Einstein); Thomas Marent: 78–79; PA Photos: Ben Margot / AP 157cla; Reuters:
Claro Cortes 157fcla

All other images © Dorling Kindersley
For further information see: www.dkimages.com

Designed and typeset by Dorling Kindersley in 11.5/15.5 Bembo
Printed and bound by South China Printing Co. Ltd

**Discover more at
www.dk.com**

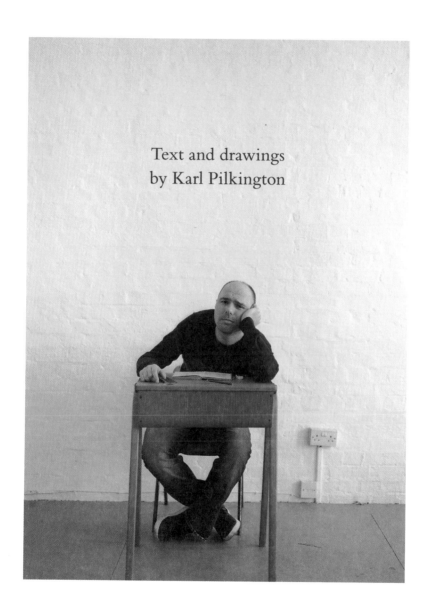

Text and drawings
by Karl Pilkington

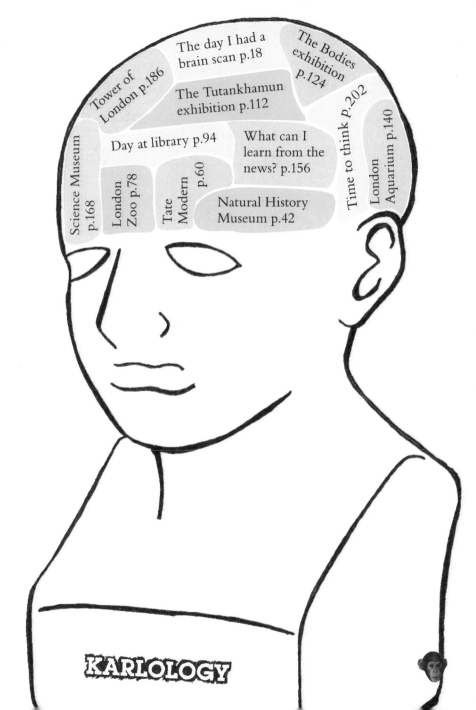

KARLOLOGY

Foreword

They say the more you know, the more you know you don't know. I don't know who first said this (which proves the saying is right), and I don't know who came up with this one either: "All we know is still infinitely less than all that still remains unknown". It's comments like these that put me off trying to learn.

I don't know if I'm cut out to be really intelligent. We're all born with a brain, but are we all born with the same quality of brain?

Then again, it's easy to blame the brain but sometimes it's my eyes that are lazy. When I try to read facts or information, my eyes drift away onto something else, so the chance of having my eyes working and my brain interested at the same time is small. Then there's my ears: they might hear something that tells the brain to stop reading and tells the eyes to go and have a look at what the ears heard. I don't know which one of these senses makes the main decisions in my life.

Maybe this is why I don't know much.

Karl will never be a high-flier

THERE'S A FAMOUS QUOTE that goes something like "Show me the boy at seven and I'll show you the man". Mrs Mathews, my infant school head teacher, thought she could do that, but she couldn't. Though she might have been right if she'd said it about John Totton, the school midget, as I'm guessing he didn't change his looks that much. "Karl will never be a high-flier" was what she said to me mam and dad at my first parents' evening. Some kids would take that comment as a challenge and go on to try to prove her wrong, but my brain decided to deal with it by going on strike.

I don't think anyone in that school was gonna be a high-flier. The kids hated being there and so did the teachers. I put it down to the state of the school. I don't think I'm exaggerating when I say the Colosseum in Rome is in better condition than some of them classrooms were. The fact the school was knocked down in 1979 and the Colosseum is still standing is evidence of this.

The school was a right mess. It must have been built on the cheap in the late 50s or early 60s. It was made from more wood than brick and was placed in the middle of a big field, with the council estate where I grew up on one side, and a big chemical plant and swamp surrounded by electricity pylons (that gave off a constant loud buzz) on the other. I don't know what sort of chemicals they were knocking out at the plant, but in every assembly we were told by Mrs Mathews to stay away from the field's boundaries. We never knew why this was so important until one morning when she brought out a pupil who'd got too close to the boundary and had burnt his face on the grass. To this day I don't know what it was that caused his burns, but for years I thought that's why there were "keep off the grass" signs in parks.

There was also a major problem with flies coming from the swamp. It got so bad one hot summer that our homework was to come up with ways to keep flies out of the classroom. I asked me dad for help. His advice was "put a bucket of shit in the corridor". He then told me how a mate of his put an advert in the local newspaper years ago that read, "Guaranteed to get rid of unwanted flies. Works 100%. Send payment to receive your fly killing kit NOW". People sent the payment and all he sent back to them was a small block of wood and some instructions that read, "Place fly on block of wood and hit with hammer. (Hammer not included.)" Me dad said the bloke got away with it as it did work if you could get hold of the fly.

I came up with Sellotape sprinkled with sugar. I don't like killing things, so this seemed like a nicer way for them to go as at least they'd have a nice meal before they died – a bit like prisoners on death row. Most kids just took in cans of fly spray. I think the class of '79 single-handedly did in the ozone layer with all them CFC gases. Like I say, I don't think any pupils who went to that school learnt much from being there, but maybe now, due to the chemical plant, poisonous grass and intake of fly spray, a few of them now have superpowers.

For the few years I was there, I can't recall seeing a caretaker. That job was done by kids held back after school for being naughty. Instead of doing lines or reading a book, they'd re-putty windows or rub down and paint door frames. I was held back twice and told to weed the playground. There were some jobs that kids weren't qualified to do – like repairing holes in the roof and walls – so they were just left to get worse, which meant that some of the school's rooms could only be used in certain weather. I was at that school for two or three years before they knocked it down, and apart from one hot summer I don't think I ever took my coat off.

As music was probably seen as the least important subject, music lessons were done in one of the worst rooms (that's if they weren't already cancelled due to the teacher being off with flu). It was so freezing in that room, the maracas shook on their own. Religious education was another subject that didn't seem to be taken seriously, as the lessons were mainly done in the cloakroom. (The space may as well have been used for something – seeing as nobody ever took their coat off.) It was hard for us to understand why there was so much fuss about Jesus being born in a stable when here we were sat somewhere equally as grim. To make the space a bit more bearable, the cloakroom was also where the school pets were kept. Most schools had a hamster or a gerbil, but Mrs Mathews decided terrapins might be more at home in our school due to the cooler, damper conditions. But I think it was too damp as they seemed to go all mouldy, and the school had to get rid of them in the end as some kids got really sick from handling them.

English was the most important lesson of all and was

done in the best quality room. When I say best quality, I mean a room with a decent roof. It was still a cold room, though. Mrs Carol taught us English and history and came up with songs and dances to help us memorize spellings. I don't think the dancing helped towards the spelling – it was probably added just to help us stay warm. I used to think the school in the American TV series *Fame* had the same heating problem, with all the dancing they did. Thinking about it now, I wonder if Mrs Carol trained to be a music teacher but didn't like the state of the room and so went for English and history instead. The fact that she had a rusty tambourine and had us singing "Rasputin" by Boney M for our history lesson is more evidence of this.

News got out that kids were doing the caretaker's job when Simon Reeves burnt his hand with some paint stripper and his mam made a song and dance of it (I'm surprised Mrs Carol didn't beat her to it) and went to the local newspaper. The council visited the school and did a health and safety check, and within about a week we were all given a letter for our parents explaining that the school was going to be knocked down. I used to always lose these notes, so I just told my dad what I remembered the note saying, which was that they were knocking the school down due to problems with albatross. He didn't believe me, so called the school to find that the problem was in fact asbestos.

All the singing that Mrs Carol made us do has stayed with me. I still use the singing method when remembering times tables, the alphabet and phone numbers. I've always said I could never be an actor cos I'd never remember all my lines, but I reckon I'd be alright in an opera. Mrs Carol's favourite words to sing about were the places Constantinople and Mississippi. Not the most popular or useful words to learn, but catchy in a song. I think this is the first time I've ever written them down since learning them. I've got no plans to visit these places, but even if I was to go, it's up to the pilot to spell it properly as he's the one who has to type it into his sat nav system.

And since I was never going to be a "high-flier", that was never going to be my job.

* * *

I left school in 1988 and didn't bother picking up my exam results as I'd already got myself a job at a printers. (I left school earlier than everyone else so I could beat all the other kids who would also be looking for work.) It wasn't until around 2001, when I was producing a radio show for Ricky Gervais and Stephen Merchant, that I found out my results.

Ricky and Stephen couldn't believe that I never bothered to find out how I got on, so they made a few calls and found that all I got was an E in History.

Even though the results don't matter any more, it's always bothered me a little that I never learnt that much from my school years. So in 2008 I thought I would try to learn as much as I could by visiting places and meeting people I could learn from, to see if having lots of knowledge is all it's cracked up to be.

THE DAY I HAD

"There is a foolish corner in the brain of the wisest man."
Aristotle

A BRAIN

SCAN

The day I had a brain scan

I THINK THE BRAIN is the weirdest thing in the body, and it's probably the ugliest thing as well. I don't feel bad about saying that cos it's *my* brain that came up with it. It doesn't like the look of itself, to the point that it tells me not to eat anything that looks like a brain either. I don't like cauliflower, cos that's kind of brain-looking, and I've always got rid of the walnut off the top of a Walnut Whip before eating it. Coincidence?

I've wondered if I'm in charge of the brain or if the brain is in charge of me. After a bit of thought and people-watching, I came to the conclusion that the brain is in charge. It came to me when I saw some people getting on their push-bikes. The first thing they did was put on a bike helmet, which to me is a sign that the brain is just looking after itself. It doesn't tell you to look after your knees or elbows by wearing pads, it just tells you to look after *it*, so that's why I think the brain is in charge. Mind you, it wants me to think that doesn't it.

An odd thing about my brain is that it sometimes plays tricks on me. A few months ago, I was waiting for the tube on the London Underground. There was me and three others – a middle-aged woman, a young lad and an old fella who looked about seventy – all within about 8 foot of each other. The old man was sat next to me. I was looking at a poster on the platform that was advertising Scotland as a great place to visit. The poster had a view of some sort of tunnel coming out of a mountain, which I didn't think was the best image of Scotland to get tourists to visit. I noticed the old man was also looking at it, so I said, "That doesn't make me want to visit Scotland". He totally ignored me. The other two people didn't flinch either. I was so ignored that I actually wondered if I'd said it. It's like that question about a tree falling in the woods – if no one is there, does it make a sound? Even though my brain thought it had made me speak, without confirmation from one of the other people on the platform, it couldn't be sure that I'd actually said it out loud.

The other problem with my brain is that it isn't always interested in the same things as me. I'll enjoy reading about something but then have problems remembering any of it, so I normally tell my girlfriend Suzanne about it as soon as possible, so she can remember it for me. Then if my brain blanks it out, I just ask her what was the amazing thing that I told her. I use her brain like a backup drive that you have for a computer.

As I mentioned earlier, I didn't do well in my exams at school so I decided to take a Mensa test to see if my brain had got any better with age. The test took place in a university building in London at 6:30 pm. This worried me cos my brain slows down as the day goes on. It's brilliant from about 8:15 am until 9:45-ish. After that, it's all downhill.

There was me and twelve others. Odd bunch of people. They all seemed to know each other. I heard two of them talking about recent science news that surgeons had been able to keep a heart beating even though it wasn't connected to a body. I thought this was a waste of heartbeats and energy. It's like going out and leaving the TV on. We're constantly being told to save energy, and yet surgeons are leaving hearts pumping.

I think we're getting too clever when it comes to health. We're saving too many people and we're living too long.

What I've learnt

If you were to count, at a rate of one thing per second, everything that happened in your brain in just one second, it would take you 32 million years.

Danny Wallace

When I was younger, there was always someone ill in the family who we'd visit and give grapes to, but I haven't done that for years. Now grape sales are on their arse. You solve one problem and it creates another. Years ago people made do with what they were dealt with when it came to health. I recently read about a fella named the Lighthouse Man who had a big hole in the top of his head. He never moaned about it or had surgery – instead he decided to make use of it and stuck a candle in it so he could wander about at night without putting a light on. So not only did he not hassle doctors to try to sort it, he was also energy efficient.

Everyone sat down ready to take the Mensa test. I took the last seat that was available. The others had all brought lots of pencils and their own stopwatches; I had to borrow a pen from the Mensa rep. This caused the others to tut.

The test began. It was tough, but the questions were multiple choice so I went with my gut feeling at first. After a while, though, even my gut was starting to say pass. The test was broken into three papers, so we had a break between each one. The others seemed quite calm with it all and chatted with each other in the breaks. One woman was even doing Sudoku in the break. She couldn't get enough.

People love to be tested these days. Every time I put the telly on, there's someone asking me a question on *Who*

Wants to be a Millionaire, *Eggheads* or *The Weakest Link*. Me Aunty Nora tried to grow a bonsai plant just cos she'd heard Alan Titchmarsh say they're hard to grow. Everyone seems to like a challenge. My brain prefers the easy life.

The really odd thing was, none of the people taking the test ever seemed to laugh. It made me wonder if intelligent

people need laughter. I thought about this more on the way home. Maybe the brain doesn't really like laughing. Mad people who have faults with their brain laugh a lot, and babies whose brains haven't grown properly love a good laugh, but it seems that normal brains don't have time for having a laugh. Another example is how you can't tickle yourself. The brain doesn't let you do it. When I have had the odd laughing fit, it's normally my brain that has to step in and put a stop to it by thinking of serious things.

I got my Mensa results a few weeks later. They were a joke, but again, my brain didn't laugh.

Anyway, I decided that for this chapter it would be good to have a picture of my brain because, at the end of the day, it's that that's come up with what I'm telling you. I found a lad on the internet who could get his hands on an MRI scanning machine. He said he could get me some good shots of my brain.

I like to think about my brain a lot (which proves it loves itself as well as being in charge), but I can't get me head around how the brain was created. I can grasp how humans might have developed from fish over time, but it's the brain bit that gets me. Scientists always use the evolution argument when they don't know how things have grown an extra leg or learnt to fly, but I don't understand how the brain could evolve. Evolve from what? I have a theory that the brain might have come from another planet where brains ruled. A planet where there was no atmosphere and the brains just floated around thinking about stuff all day. They quickly became advanced because of the amount of thinking being done. Then, somehow, they came to planet Earth but found they were useless because they couldn't move about by floating any more. So one of the brainier ones got into a monkey's head ... and the rest is history. Like I say, it's just a theory.

Six days after emailing the lad about the brain scan, there I was in a bunker deep below a London university (not far from where I took my Mensa test) with Hugo and Joe and a million-pound camera. Joe explained how it worked, I pretended I understood. If he'd taken a picture of what my brain was doing at that point, he would have seen it overheating. I could tell that Joe loved that machine. He said stuff like, "There's plenty of elbow room, more than 27 inches from side to side for a more comfortable shoulder, chest or upper abdomen scan". He was the Jeremy Clarkson of scanning machines: "True comfort and quality – some patients drift off to sleep, it's so comfortable". If the medical profession doesn't work out for Joe, he could easily get a job on QVC flogging these scanners. He told me

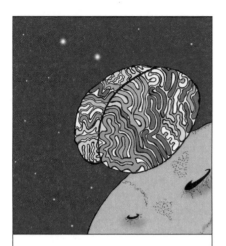

There was a planet where only brains existed. They did nothing but float about and think about stuff.

One of the brainier brains had had enough and escaped from brain planet and landed on Earth.

Only problem was, it couldn't float about on Earth like it could on its own planet. It had been using all its brain power to plan the journey route and went and forgot about the gravity problem.

The brain sat thinking, as that's all it could do. Until a chimp came along.

The brain noticed that the chimp was a bit gormless but was able to move around. Luckily the chimp has massive ears so the brain decided to use up all the power it had to climb up and into the ears when the gormless chimp was asleep.

There wasn't much else in the head, so the brain had room to sit quite happily, and within no time the chimp was being guided by the brain.

Something else that is quite weird is the way that a chimps arse looks similar to the brain. I wonder if another brain attempted to get into the chimp via the bum, and the way it looks now is a hangover from that. Just another theory.

how they're getting more and more powerful. I said they'll have to stop at some point, though, or they'll get to a point where they see right through the head altogether, which would be pointless.

I started to feel a bit nervous about coming face to face with my brain, or was it my brain that felt nervous about me seeing it? I get like this whenever I have any sort of medical test as the doctors always seem to find something. That's what doctors do. They're like archaeologists who keep digging until they hit bone, or car mechanics who always find something that needs replacing. So I prefer to leave it for as long as possible before having a check-up. The last time I went to the doctor's was because Suzanne told me to get a wart checked. I went to the walk-in clinic in Soho and explained at the reception that I had a wart my girlfriend was worried about. They sent me through to the nurse, who read on the note that I had a wart. Without even making eye contact, she asked me to drop my trousers. She was sat down, I was stood up. She stared at my bits for a few moments and did that thing people with glasses do where they squint and then look over the top of the glasses, as if she was studying a piece of art.

"I'm having problems locating it", she said.

"It's here on the side of my face."

"Oh … okay. Pull your trousers up."

She explained that most cases of warts in the Soho clinic were of a sexual nature. She gave me some cream to put on it and the wart fell off within a week, which made me glad that the wart wasn't on me nob.

I suppose I should have queried her asking me to drop my pants, but I don't like questioning doctors as I don't want to annoy them. The same goes for builders or plumbers – I don't like to quiz them either, for two reasons: (1) cos I don't want them to get annoyed as they'll probably end up charging me more or do a duff job on purpose; and (2) cos I can't speak Polish.

Another reason I get nervous is because I hear too much about what can go wrong with the body. That's why I think having knowledge can be a bad thing. It can worry you. A mate's mate told me how someone he knew banged his head in a car crash, survived, had no loss of memory, but his brain went gay. Which is weird cos I've heard that banging your head makes you lose calories, and seeing as most gays I see knocking about look like fitness freaks, their gayness might be due to head-banging their calories away. Again – just a theory.

There was another story about a woman who had "alien hand syndrome". This is when people with epilepsy have the two halves of the brain separated to stop seizures happening. The woman could still feel things with her hands, but she couldn't control one of them. It ended up doing things of its own accord. She was a smoker, but the weird hand wasn't happy with this and used to grab the cigs from her mouth and throw them away before her normal hand could light them. She said it's the most annoying thing that could happen to anyone, but I reckon having a leg that

Things the woman with alien-hand syndrome couldn't do ...

Swimming

Boxing

walks where you don't want to go would be a lot worse.

These sorts of things are a doctor's dream as it makes a change from looking at boils, coughs and warts. I watched one of them programmes where they cover stories about people who've got stuff stuck in their ear or up their nose, and one of the incidents involved a bloke who went to the doctor's to report a headache that wouldn't go away. The doctor decided to take an X-ray and found he had eleven nails in his head. The doctor took them out and the fella was fine and the headaches went away. Doctors love a challenge like this. Taking them nails out would have been like having a game of Kerplunk to that doctor.

It's the weird stuff that excites doctors. Chinese surgeons

Hairdressing   Juggling

are the best in the world cos they're always dealing with kids with four legs or two heads in China, but Chinese doctors are rubbish when it comes to getting rid of a rash or a cold. There's a Chinese medicine shop round the corner from where I live and they give you twigs and leaves to eat if you have some eczema or flu. This shows the Chinese are not as up-to-date with everyday illnesses, yet they are great when it comes to removing an extra head.

As Joe did the final checks on the scanner, he told me how he had his eye on a new model of scanner, the fMRI. This new machine can actually see your thoughts take place and can show you what thoughts go on where in the brain, whereas I was only having an ordinary MRI. I was

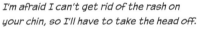

I'm afraid I can't get rid of the rash on your chin, so I'll have to take the head off.

glad about this as it would be weird them knowing what was going on in my head. I had a similar experience when I worked at a recording studio where I made cassettes. A mind-reading woman had made some audio tapes of her explaining how to mind read. She turned up to collect them with her pet dog and I hadn't finished doing them yet, so she said she would wait. I was about to think how much of a pain in the arse she was for not just popping back in ten minutes when I thought I can't do that, cos she'd know what I was thinking! So I came up with a quick plan. I decided to think about dog food and being happy running down a beach after a ball, so that she would think she was picking up thoughts from the mind of her pet dog. Stressful day's work, that was.

"Is there any danger involved?" I asked Joe.

He said no, but then asked me to sign a consent form.

Before I knew it, I was being slid into the machine like a Sunday joint being popped into an oven. I had a few little panic attacks while I was inside. My brain started to think that the fillings in my teeth were getting hot. I don't really like tight spaces or the feeling of being trapped. I can't use sleeping bags cos of the trapped feeling, and this was worse. I tried to relax but the noise from the machine was loud. He'd said earlier that people sometimes nod off inside the

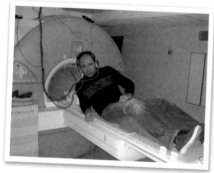

scanner, but I don't know how. I felt like a sock in a washing machine.

I think most people's brains are like mine, but then you get the odd good one that changes the world. You've got people who can tell where dinosaurs walked on Earth and what they had for their last meal 65 million years ago, and yet the doughnut who works at the service company in charge of our flat can't tell me whether our windows are gonna get cleaned in the next month. There are more idiots in the world than bright ones, but it's the odd good one that makes a big difference. I still can't explain how gravity works, yet Isaac Newton worked it out years ago. He came up with loads of other intelligent stuff as well, but everyone only remembers the gravity theory he came up with while he was sat under a tree and an apple fell on his head. It's probably well-known cos it's a good anecdote, but fancy sitting under a tree that has apples falling off it. It just goes to show that he was good with maths, but he had no common sense. Same goes for Archimedes. He came up with loads of theories but is mainly known for running down the street naked shouting "Eureka!" after having a good idea in the bath. I think it's harder to come up with ideas and solutions now. If these people were around today, they'd struggle. Newton wouldn't be allowed to sit under an apple tree cos there'd probably be a "keep off the grass" sign, or apple trees would have fences round them to stop people nicking the apples. Archimedes wouldn't have a bath, due to water shortage, and would be advised to have a shower cos it's better for the environment. And as for running down the street naked, he'd be banged up. Things have changed.

Fourteen minutes later the scan was over. Joe came in and pulled me out of the machine and removed the cage from around my head. I felt like a magician's assistant who'd been cut in half and then put back together again. He told me it would take a few hours to get the scans developed, so I used this time to talk to Hugo about the brain. I don't remember everything he said, apart from how the brain of the elephant is the largest in size among the land mammals (elephants always look sad, which proves my point about how intelligence and laughter don't like each other) and that telling lies is a complicated thing for the brain to do. I'm not very good at lying. The first lie that I remember telling was to me mam when she found an apple in the fruit bowl that had been bitten and put back. I said the cat did it. Another was when I bought some knock-off Adidas trainers from a mate at school for £10.

"Why are they so cheap?" me mam asked. "Is it cos they're stolen?"

"No. They're cheap cos the lad's dad owns the company", I lied. I thought it was quite a good one.

"What's his name?"

"Simon Adidas", I said.

Like I say, I'm not that good at lies.

To lie well, you have to have a really good brain and memory. JK Rowling must be a right good liar to write all those Harry Potter books about a made-up wizard and keep them believable. The problem with that is, she's so good at lying I wouldn't trust her as far as I could throw her.

Hugo brought up the images of my brain on his computer. It was weird to see it. It was like seeing someone you've spoken to a lot on the phone but never met face to face. I knew what it thought about stuff, but I'd never seen it. I thought it was quite a good-looking brain, but maybe I thought this cos it belongs to me. It's like when people have a baby scan and the owners think it's beautiful, when to other people it just looks like a frog.

Hugo told me it's important to keep the brain healthy by

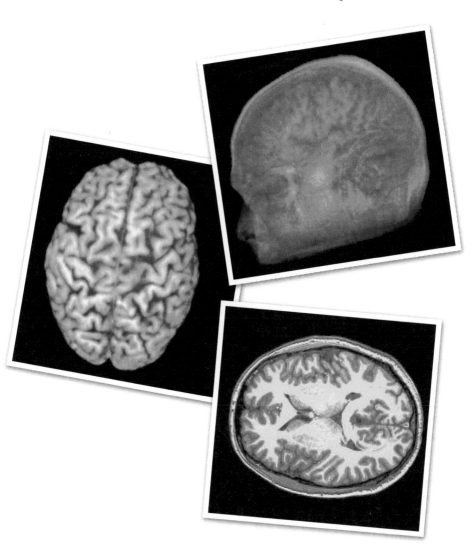

keeping it active and eating well. "Omega-3 fats are good for the brain", he said. When I got home I looked on-line to see which foods contain this stuff. I found it's in walnuts. My brain doesn't like walnuts.

BRAIN FACTS

The human brain is pink, has the consistency of blancmange, and contains 100 billion brain cells along which thoughts travel at 250 mph. The number of possible circuits the brain cells can make with each other is greater than the number of atoms in the Universe.

The brain can end up doing some odd things. These are some of the illnesses people get when the brain doesn't work properly:

<u>Face blindness</u> (prosopagnosia) – this means you can't recognize faces.

<u>Cotard delusion</u> – you believe you are either non-existent or dead.

<u>Capgras syndrome</u> – your brain makes you think your family have been replaced by identical imposters.

<u>Intermetamorphosis</u> – you think people swap identities while keeping their original bodies.

<u>Mirrored self-misidentification</u> – the only symptom here is that you can't recognize yourself in the mirror.

IS · MX · NO

ES · FI · HK · IS
SK · UK · ZA

E · BR · CA · CH
EE · ES · FI · FR
IE · IS · IT · LT
NL · NO · NZ
G · SI · UK · ZA

Charles Darwin *'It is not the strongest of the species that survive,*

nor the most intelligent,

but the ones most responsive to change."

Natural History Museum

IT'S GOOD THAT WE EVOLVED from some sort of sea creature and grew a brain, but I think it's a shame that we couldn't have grown a decent brain whilst at the same time staying in the sea. I think this is when evolution took a wrong turn and started going downhill. Getting out of the sea was our biggest mistake.

Earth is known as the blue planet for a reason, the reason being that it's 70% water, and that's without even counting all the swimming pools. Even swimming pools are getting bigger and deeper than they used to be. When I was younger, pools used to always have a bit of space around them, but now, due to the amount of water on the planet, we have invented infinity pools where there is no longer a gap. We're running out of ways of using the water up. I think this is why they tell us to drink at least two litres a day – not cos it's good for us, but just so the planet doesn't drown itself.

It's simple, we should have never left the sea. No fish is homeless, no fish dies of starvation or stress. But cos we got out of the sea, we now have these problems. We have to work to pay for a house or a flat to live in, we have to pay for food, we have to pay for electric/gas to keep us warm. Then, if we're lucky, if any money is left over, what do we do? We use it to go for holidays back at the place we should never have left to begin with. The sea.

We're panicking now cos they say the sea levels are rising and land will start disappearing, but if we'd stayed as fish that would be good news, as we could spread out a bit, have a few different rocks to live under in different parts of the new extended sea. They also say we are running out of cod and that we should stop eating it, but I think we're not running out – I think the cod is just harder to find with all this new water that's been added from the melting icebergs. Me Aunty Nora is worried about the melting icebergs, not cos of rising sea levels but cos she thinks that's where we get our ice from, and she can't drink whisky and coke without ice as it gives her heartburn.

Anyway, problem is we can't go back now – we've lost all them skills we would have had as fish. I can only do the breaststroke for a few metres before I'm out of breath.

I feel like we've messed up, like nature is no longer in charge of our destiny. Proof of this is the labradoodle. It's a new dog we've knocked up that's a cross between a labrador and a poodle. (It's so new that the spell check on my computer is asking me to check the spelling as I type this, as it's never heard of a labradoodle.) It's aimed at people who like the character of the labrador but aren't keen on its hairstyle.

I thought for this chapter, a trip to the Natural History Museum was in order to see what nature had put together over the years.

It was all going to plan. I'd got up early and was at the museum fifteen minutes before opening time. There was me and twelve others waiting outside. "I'll get in and out of the dinosaur section before all the kids on their school trips even get off the bus", is what I'd thought. I got in there and looked at the map. Chinese art, glass art, medieval sculptures, fashion, photography.

"Where have you put the dinosaurs?" I asked the old security man.

"Dinosaurs? You won't find any dinosaurs in here, you want the Natural History Museum."

Turns out I was in the V&A. I don't know why they have all the museums so close together. The V&A, the Natural History Museum and the Science Museum are all within five minutes of each other. If another meteorite hits Earth and wipes out all civilization, then in billions of years time, when humans grow back again, some archaeologist is gonna be well confused when they start digging round here and find human bones, dinosaur bones, bits of old Chinese art, odd fashion, polar bears, dodos, fish and computers all within a 1-mile radius.

Who knows, maybe that's what happened last time. Maybe the dinosaurs we found aren't real and never existed – it could just have been some weird artist fella who made sculptures out of mammoth bones. If the world does get hit by a big meteorite again and someone in the future finds Damien Hirst's shark in a tank of formaldehyde, future people might think we kept sharks as pets.

I shot off to the Natural History Museum. It was too late. Three coach-loads of kids had just emptied and the queue was massive. To try and get in there now would be pointless, so I went to find a café. It's quite a posh area that the museums are in, so I ended up in a French café where

I had a coffee. As I said at the beginning of the chapter, everything has evolved, even coffee. You can't just ask for a coffee any more as there are so many different species of it. Espresso, latte, mocha, Americano and many others. I had a cappuccino and a thing called a gourmande. It sounds fancy, but to describe a gourmande in English, I'd say it's a roll of gooey, fatty pastry with some soft melted chocolate in it. Food is something else that is forever changing, which in turn changes us. I think in years to come, the human jaw will become really weak as we don't eat really tough stuff any more, plus we talk less due to text and email. The jaw will become weak, then teeth will be next. Wisdom teeth are what's left over from our animal days when we had to tackle tough meat, but these are no longer needed due to people blending everything. Most of our food is now soft. We have smoothies; soft bread; when Suzanne buys an avocado she looks for a soft one; and then you've got Softmints. I remember when I was a kid in the 80s eating Wham bars that could take a week to get through and would give your jaw a proper workout. I think they were invented to keep kids quiet, cos after eating one your jaw was too tired to talk. They should make them again and chuck them in the sea to bring shark attacks down, as they'd be too weak to tackle a human after a Wham bar.

Those days of strong human jaws are gone, and we're now weaker then ever. It's not just our jaws, it's everything. Years ago we only needed "an apple a day to keep the doctor away", but now they say eat five pieces of fruit. Either that or we've just got way too much fruit. There is fruit that is still unknown to me. People say it's good we have all this fruit on offer, but I think it's just made it harder to win on fruit machines cos the chances of getting three the same is now impossible. It was easy in the days when there were just plums, melons and cherries, but there's loads more than that now.

The nose will disappear in time as well, as we don't use it any more to smell food and check if it's off – we just rely on "use-by dates" instead. These are probably also making the stomach weak by stopping us from challenging it to handle something that's a little bit off or out of date. I also think it's these dates that are making more people obese, as people are eating food not cos they're hungry but cos they don't want to chuck it in the bin due to the use-by date.

Anyway, I went back to the museum. There were even more coaches outside and the queue hadn't really gone down, so I had no choice but to join it. In front of me was a fat lad with two of his mates. He was a goth and wore a mixed-up selection of clothes. He had dark make-up round his eyes, a top hat, a long black leather coat, red chequered trousers and a T-shirt with the band Nightwish on the front. He was eating a big bag of Revels (mixed-up toffees to go with his mixed-up clothes). Before I knew it, I was at the front of the queue and had spent £4 for a guide before I'd even got me foot inside the place.

Everyone seemed to be going into the dinosaur section, so I went to the quieter areas first. The first thing I saw was an old handaxe dated back to 300,000 years ago. It said that the tool may have been used to "kill and build" with – a tool that Black & Decker is yet to bring out. It said there were no other items found lying around near the axe. A tidy builder, I thought. That's something else that's become extinct.

They had nearly every animal you can think of in the Natural History Museum. In a way, it's better than the zoo cos there are more animals, plus they are all stuffed, so they can't wander off and hide somewhere to have a kip like they do in the zoo. As well as the chubby goth wearing a top hat, I saw some other things at the Natural History Museum that I'd never seen before, like wombats, yaks, the sloth bear, a skeleton of a dodo, an antler off a giant deer, and a flying fox bat, which was the spitting image of a normal fox but this one had grown wings. This might be nature's way of saving the fox from becoming extinct. I think wings are the best thing to grow. The giraffe drew the short straw when it was given a long neck to survive, I'd much prefer wings. A mate told me that the giraffe got a long neck due to having to stretch for food. The way Asda's shelves are getting higher and higher, I think we might go the same way.

I read about the sivathere, which was around years and years ago but no longer exists. They say it was a cross between a giraffe and a moose. I don't think that mix was ever needed on the world, and that's why they died out. (Labradoodle will go for similar reasons.) Not having a purpose finishes you off. This is why you hear about old people dying two weeks after retirement – it's cos they feel useless. I think this is the same reason why I went bald. The hair on my head never felt needed. I never styled it well or did anything special with it, so it felt useless and fell out. This is also why the sivathere wasn't about for long. I don't even remember hearing if Noah tried to get two of them on his boat, so even he must have thought they were a daft idea.

There was a fish section where they had some things I'd read about on a visit to the London Aquarium. There was a thing called the rat-trap fish, named cos its mouth has no floor, so the jaw can snap shut without water slowing it down. They also had a stuffed angler fish, which I've always wanted to see. These are the fish that live so deep down in the sea that they have a built-in light system so they glow in the dark. But the ones I saw were dead, so there were no lights. They don't look that impressive without the lights. Bit like Blackpool in a power cut. These are also the fish that have a stomach that can expand so it can eat things bigger than themselves. They had one that hadn't eaten before it died, and then there was one that had, to show you how much they can expand. It was like one of them

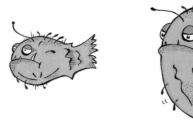

before-and-after pictures you get in magazines advertising Weight Watchers. It was well weird, I never thought I'd see a fish with cellulite. This could be another reason for sea levels rising – if there's now loads of fat fish knocking about, sea levels go up. Archimedes would agree with me on that one.

I made my way back to the dinosaur section. In the middle of the hall was a massive, full-size replica skeleton of a *Diplodocus*. *Diplodocus* was wandering around on Earth about 145 million years ago. They were huge in size (26 metres in length) but were quiet, calm creatures who spent their time in herds plodding about just eating. Sounds a bit like the goth I saw on the way in. It's always the big stuff that seems to be in danger of dying out. Dinosaurs, whales, pandas and polar bears. I suppose being big isn't all it's cracked up to be. I can safely say I have never seen a midget involved in an accident or in a doctor's waiting room, so maybe being small is best. It kinda makes sense – if you're not taking up as much room, there's less chance of a germ finding you.

The guide said that the museum staff call the *Diplodocus* "Dippy". Humans love naming stuff. When a whale got lost and ended up getting stuck in the River Thames, everyone started coming up with names for it quicker than they came up with solutions to save it. When I was looking on the internet about dinosaurs, I read that a T. rex found in Montana was named "Thomas the T. Rex". We love naming stuff so much that it'll get to a point where you go to the Doctor's and he says, "I'm afraid you've got a touch of 'Colin the Cancer' in your lungs".

It said that, for years, the museum displayed the *Diplodo-*

cus tail dragging on the ground, until new research showed these dinosaurs probably carried their tails up in the air. So they've now lifted it up by attaching wires from the ceiling. I don't know if they really did do the research or if people kept tripping over it and the museum came up with this story to get it out of the way. Makes me wonder if T. rex really did stand on its two back legs as they suggested, or is this another thing they made up so it took up less floor space so they could open the expensive café.

There was information about the different ways people think dinosaurs may have become extinct. There was the asteroid theory, severe ice age, contagious disease, a giant volcano, and they recently found a dinosaur that had evidence of parasites living inside it, which may have finished it off. It's things like parasites that make me hope reincarnation doesn't happen. I wouldn't mind coming back as a dog or a budgie, but a parasite? What a grim existence that is. I watched a programme about tapeworms. Horrible things, they are. They spend more time living inside something else's body than they spend in the outside world, and then their last few moments of life are spent coming out of someone's arse. It's not great is it?

When I was younger we had a cat. Well, we had a lot of cats as we lived on a main road and got through them quickly, but one of them jumped on the table and I noticed something hanging from its backside. I told me dad and he had a look and said it looked like a tapeworm. Me mam put some rubber cleaning gloves on and grabbed it. It stretched to about two foot. The cat didn't look happy. It was using it's claws to cling to the crack in the table as me mam pulled the thing out. It eventually left the cat. Turned out it wasn't a tapeworm but an elastic band that the cat must have eaten.

However the dinosaurs were wiped out, the chances are it will happen again and wipe us out. I'm sure we can slow down the ageing process of the Earth a little, by using less energy and all that, but the world is still getting old and we can't stop that. No matter how much anti-ageing cream a woman puts on her face, or how much plastic surgery she has, she can't escape getting old and looking grim. I think this is why nature makes sure we lose our sight as we get older – it's so we don't leave our old partners and try and get something newer. I think the reason divorce numbers are up is cos of the invention of glasses and contact lenses.

It is taken as fact that man wasn't around at the same time as the dinosaurs, but I don't think it's impossible. I

What I've learnt

Sticklebacks normally flee a heron's shadow. However, there is a parasite that starts its life cycle in the fish but needs to get into a warm-blooded animal to complete that cycle. So what it actually does is change the stickleback's behavior. Now the fish doesn't flee the bird's shadow, so it gets eaten. The parasite ends up inside the warm-blooded bird and can complete its cycle.

Ricky Gervais

know there isn't evidence as they haven't found any skeletons or fossils, but with the amount of building work that goes on everywhere, I think it's only a matter of time before they find something that proves we were around together. It could just be hard to find because the dinosaurs ate most of the humans and left no trace, or cos man's skeletons are smaller than that of a *Diplodocus*. It's like when you play computer battleships – it's always easier to hit the aircraft carrier than it is to find the torpedo boat. Maybe we were around but there just wasn't that many of us, a bit like pug dogs – they've been around for years but I only saw one for the first time about nine years ago. I don't think it would have been impossible to live with dinosaurs either. They say the most dangerous things on the planet now are mosquitoes as they can carry loads of killer diseases and bite you when you're asleep without you realising it. Mosquitoes wouldn't be that much of a problem to us if we hadn't left the sea.

NATURAL HISTORY FACTS

Scientists have discovered and named about 1.2 million species of animals. Of these, three-quarters are insects. Of the insects, a third are beetles.

For every individual person alive today, there are 200 million insects.

The insect with the shortest adult life is the female American sand-burrowing mayfly. She dies of old age after five minutes.

The coffin fly spends nearly its whole life cycle inside buried coffins, where it feeds and breeds on decomposing human flesh.

Although insects are the world's most successful animals, none live in the sea. Only a few have colonized the human body, including lice and botflies. Botflies spend the first part of their life-cycle as maggots burrowing into human flesh.

The ringworm parasite is not a worm but a type of mould that grows in the decomposing outer layer of dead skin on a living person's body.

The largest parasite of the human body is the beef tapeworm, which can grow to 65 feet long.

Grasshoppers sometimes jump into swimming pools and drown because they are driven to suicide by a parasite. The hairworm parasite grows inside the grasshopper until it fills the body. Then it releases chemicals that brainwash the grasshopper and make it leap into water, where the grasshopper dies and the worm swims out.

The sea sponge is one of the world's simplest animals, with no head, no arms, no legs, no eyes, no sense organs and no brain. A sea sponge can be forced through a sieve and each tiny fragment will become a new individual.

"*Art is making something out of nothing and selling it.*" Frank Zappa

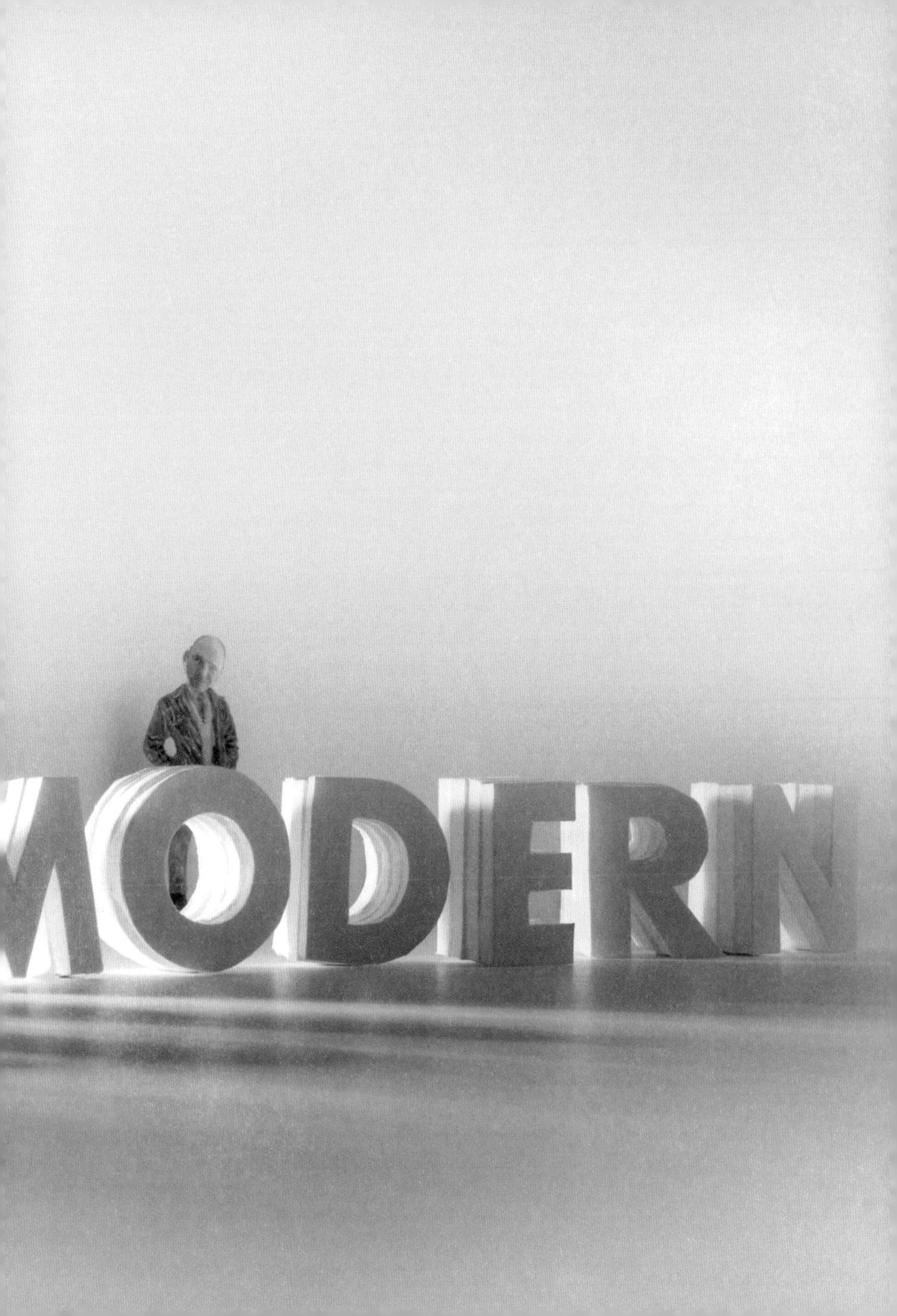
MODERN

Tate Modern

IF AN ALIEN LANDED and asked me what art was, I would find it hard to explain. I would probably say, "Art is just stuff to fill a space that would otherwise be empty". That's what we do here on planet Earth, we fill space. People buy a home which is perfectly big enough when they first move in, but then, over time, they collect so much stuff they have to get something bigger. Whatever space you have, it's never enough. Me mam and dad moved a few years ago to a house that had an old caravan in the garden. They said they'd get shut of it once they were settled in, but nine years on, the thing is still there and is now full of stuff. I don't know where all of the stuff would be if they didn't have that caravan, but this is what happens when there is space. Suzanne's mam and dad's house is the same. They've filled all the shelving units with that many knick-knacks that they've collected over the years, that stuff has now started to creep into the bathroom. You rinse your eyes under the shower whilst reaching out for the shower gel and end up rubbing your head with a pot cat. It gets really tough when I'm drying meself cos every time you waft the towel, something falls off a shelf. Last time I was there I told 'em it's like playing bleedin' Jenga in that bathroom.

I think it's in our nature to fill space. When you think about it, the human body is crammed full of stuff – every bit of it is full, not one bit of an arm or leg is hollow. Doctors say we don't need the appendix or tonsils, and men don't need nipples, but nature saw a space and filled it. We dislike the idea of empty space so much that scientists have now named nothing "nothingness", as they found that if you observe nothing, then it's no longer nothing because you were there to observe it, so nothing is actually something. Me mam and dad's house hasn't got any room to store any "nothingness" due to the amount of "somethingness".

So, art, do we need it? We like to pretend that art is really important to us cos it makes us feel individual, but when space gets tight, art is usually the first thing that gets put away. Not the TV or stereos, but art. The TV programme *Antiques Roadshow* proves this as it's full of people saying how they were cleaning out their gran's house when they found a painting by Monet stuffed under an ice-cream maker in the loft. I also think this is why art has gone smaller and smaller over the years — it's cos we no longer have room for it. Back in the 1700s you would have massive murals thirty feet across cos people lived in big houses (and didn't have TVs and stereos taking up room). Now we live in smaller places we need small art, and this is why fridge magnets were brought out. It's probably also why crime figures have gone up. Stuff is now easier to nick due to it being so small, whereas years ago, no one would've even attempted to try and nick the sculpture of David by Michelangelo. I've heard that some art is now so small that there is an artist who used a hair from a fly to paint a tiny piece that he made. This is called "micro art". This sort of art solves the space issue and also the crime problem, as the robbers can't normally find it.

I thought I'd go and look at some art to see if I could learn anything from it. I decided to go to the Tate Modern on London's South Bank. This is an area that's full of different types of art from theatre and music to paintings and sculptures. Outside the galleries were puppet shows, buskers, a man painted from head to toe in white paint (who

I presume normally acts as a statue, though he was on his lunch break when I saw him) complete with bird droppings, and the Budgie Man, who has about twelve budgies that climb ladders and dance to his own songs that he sings about budgies. There was also a homeless fella who earned cash by ripping eyes out of photos in newspapers and sticking them on his cheeks whilst covering his own eyes with a roll of toilet paper. He also had a few bird droppings on him but these weren't part of his act, they were just a consequence of sitting under bridges where pigeons live. As if that wasn't enough, he was singing Christina Aguilera's song "I am Beautiful". Everyone was loving it.

I went into the Tate Modern expecting to be charged, but it turns out the place is free. The first thing that grabbed my eye was a massive crack in the floor. This is the problem with not charging, I thought, they can't afford the upkeep of the building. Until I realized it was an exhibit. The crack was around 600 feet long, about a foot deep and went right through the exhibit hall. There was a couple of juice cartons and a Lion Bar wrapper at the bottom. I don't know if they were meant to be there or not.

I took a leaflet that explained the piece and went to the balcony above to get a better view. The leaflet said that the crack is called *Shibboleth*, which, according to the *Oxford*

English Dictionary, is "a word used as a test for detecting people from another district or country by their pronunciation; a word or a sound very difficult for foreigners to pronounce correctly". The word refers back to an incident in the Bible when the Ephraimites were trying to cross the River Jordan but got caught by their enemies the Gileadites. The Ephraimites were all forced to say the word shibboleth. Since their dialect didn't include the "sh" sound, this allowed the Gileadites to identify and slaughter large numbers of Ephraimites. The leaflet went on to say how shibboleth is "a token of power: the power to judge and kill". I took from this that the Lion Bar and drink carton weren't meant to be there.

Two Irish fellas who were stood next to me on the balcony looked at it for a while before coming to a conclusion: "That's no art. It's a load of shite". I wasn't sure if they were proper art critics, but I did know one thing for sure: they definitely weren't Ephraimites.

I watched as the crack attracted the crowds. People walked along the side of it. An old woman held onto her daughter's arm and walked carefully as if she was on the edge of the Grand Canyon. I was just thinking about how me Aunty Nora would probably fall into it on purpose to get an insurance claim in (she could then get her wish of finally getting her garden Astroturfed – she's sick of having to mow it) when a teacher shouted at one of her pupils for pushing a wheelchair-bound pupil into the crack. Security came and unlodged the wheel, while reporting back to someone on their radio that the crack wasn't damaged. The onlooking crowd did a quiet clap as if they'd just witnessed Evel

Knievel survive a jump that had gone wrong.

I enjoyed watching the people looking at the art more than the art itself. Maybe that was the point of it.

I went to see what else they had. I thought I'd treat each piece of art as if it was in a shop and I was buying something to pop in my living room. The first thing I saw was some work by an artist called Juan Muñoz. I decided pretty quickly that I wouldn't want it in my living room as it wouldn't go with anything else that I have. It was a life-size dwarf (which backs up my point about art getting smaller), made out of clay, holding a real chess set while stood on a wooden table. I stared at it for a few minutes and tried to see if it had a purpose. It didn't. It was set up like a stall at a car boot sale where the trader has tried to display their goods in a humorous way. If it was a car boot sale, I think they'd have sold the chess set and table but would be taking the dwarf back home. It looked like a novelty gift, like one of them straw donkeys wearing a hat that a friend might bring you back from Spain. It was well done though. Maybe dwarfs are hard to make cos of the different proportions. I remember the children's TV artist Tony Hart once saying that horses are difficult to draw and model cos of the odd body size and legs. He never drew a dwarf, but I imagine it would be the same problem.

I couldn't find any details on what the artist was trying to do, so I listened to other spectators discuss it. "It makes me feel a bit awkward", said a posh woman to her partner. "That little guy freaks me right out", said another. I looked at some more of Muñoz's work. There was another dwarf. Now I got the feeling he was making dwarfs just to save money on clay. The piece was called *Sara* and featured a woman dwarf looking at some pictures of herself on a snooker table. She was wearing high heels. I didn't understand it so I left.

I had been in the Tate for about an hour and hadn't really learnt anything. It's not like a visit to a museum or a show where you pick up facts – it was left to me to try and work everything out. Art seems to be about coming up with your own story or take on each piece. This made me think about the mystery of the *Mona Lisa*. Everyone likes that painting cos they don't know the story behind it. Who is she? Why the cheeky smile? If the *Mona Lisa* was done today, we'd know everything there was to know about her cos she'd have sold her story to *Heat* magazine and done some open-hearted interview with a tabloid before the paint was dry.

Another thing that's important about art is where it's placed, as it's the surroundings that can make it more interesting. That big *Angel of the North* statue in Gateshead is an example of what I mean. It's in a field off a motorway. Motorways are the most boring things to drive on, so stick something there for people to look at and they'll like it. I think that's why cavemen built Stonehenge where it is – it made the road next to it less boring to travel on.

Art was never a big deal in our house. We had lava lamps, glass clowns and ashtrays on stands. There were two paintings I can remember. One was a painting of two naked, Chinese-looking women in moonlight, called *Nymphs by Moonlight*. I think me mam's younger brother painted it. It was kept in the hall just above the chest freezer that we had at the time. The other painting was Gainsborough's *Blue Boy*, which hung in the lounge in a gold frame next to the wicker drinking bar that we had. Everyone on the estate seemed to have that picture.

Aunty Nora's house had quite a bit of art that I liked to look at as a kid (she still has it all). She had a 3D picture of a poodle that stuck its tongue out when you moved; a corkscrew with a wooden man on top, with a lever on his back that made him drink from a pint

glass; and then she had the *Crying Boy*, a painting of a young lad crying that became one of the most talked about works of art in the 1980s. From what I can remember, there was a fire in someone's house caused by a chip-pan. Everything was burnt to cinders apart from a print of the *Crying Boy*. The same incident then happened somewhere else: chip-pan fire, everything burnt, but *Crying Boy* picture intact. This started a national panic about "The Curse of the Crying Boy". Other stories were featured

in the news, including one about a woman whose husband and three older kids passed away after she bought the *Crying Boy*. She blamed the painting. More fires were reported, with the connection being the jinxed painting. People were terrified and were advised that if they owned a copy, they should remove it from their homes immediately. Thousands tried to bin it, but it got to the point where even the binmen were too scared to take them away in case the bad luck was passed on to them. So a national newspaper told its readers to send in their cursed artwork to be disposed

of properly. The paper then ran a story featuring a picture of one of their topless models wearing nowt but knickers and a fireman's helmet while she set light to a huge pile of *Crying Boy* pictures.

Nora has still got hers. I asked if it's caused any problems over the years, or if she'd experienced any weird happenings. She just said, "My feet have been a bit swollen recently". Hardly the curse of

ART

Dead artists' work shoots up in price
So am I then wrong to surmise
That the value of our flat will increase
If our painter and decorator dies

"I'm interested in expressing basic
human emotions through my choice of
colours: tragedy, ecstasy, despair, and..."

Look, will you just paint
the walls magnolia!

Tutankhamun is it.

There were loads of paintings in the Tate, to the point where my eyes got bored. I wandered from floor to floor and room to room whilst being watched by the arty-looking Tate Modern security staff, each with floppy hair and styled beard, who were ready to pounce on anyone that dared to try and rob a terracotta dwarf. My back started to ache. It does this when I've been walking for a while (it's cos I tried to kick my height when I was a kid and landed on me arse), so I went into one of the video rooms that had comfy seats. I was the only one in the room.

The video started. It was a piece called *Meat Joy* by the artist Carolee Schneemann. Half-naked women started running around with half-naked men, then they started wrestling. It looked like old 60s footage. Next some bloke comes into shot throwing dead, plucked chickens and fish onto the others while they're wrestling. I heard someone behind me. It was a young kid. His dad then followed. At this point there was a load of close-up shots of the chicken, then it panned out to reveal the chicken down a bearded man's underpants, which were being yanked by a woman. "Come on Matthew", said the dad with urgency. I felt awkward about watching the video, a lot more awkward than when I was looking at the pot midget holding a chess set. I wanted to say to the dad that I'd only popped in cos I was a bit stiff, but I didn't think that was wise. I looked back at the screen. The men and women were now wrestling while paint was being thrown around. It was like a porno version of *Tiswas*. I left before any other people came in.

I think art has gone weird like this cos everything normal has been done. Turner painted ships, Monet had images of the countryside covered, Rembrandt did good portraits, Dali did surrealism. So what's left? Naked wrestling with bald chickens. I think that's what art is about: just coming up with something that's different, and if you can stick a frame round it then all the better.

I'd had enough so I decided to leave the Tate. On the way out I passed a donation box. "If you have enjoyed your visit, please donate £3", it said. I didn't bother. Instead I gave a pound to the homeless fella who was still outside singing Christina Aguilera's "I am Beautiful". The eyes that were stuck on his cheeks earlier had now fallen off.

A few months ago I met an artist called David Shrigley. I asked him if he had any art that sums up art. He sent me this picture:

What I've learnt

One of the most useful things I have learnt is how not to open a tin of paint. It is best not to use a chisel. Once I used a chisel and stabbed myself in the palm of the hand. It was very painful. It also knackered the chisel. The best tool to use is a screwdriver. Preferably not a sharp one.

David Shrigley

ART FACTS

The world's oldest forms of art are pornographic.
Called Venus figurines, they are tiny hand-held scupFures of
female bodies with hugely enlarged breasts, thighs, hips and vulvas.

The highest price paid for a painting was $140 million in 2006,
when a Mexican financier bought Jackson Pollock's "No. 5, 1948",
one of Pollock's distinctive abstract paint splatterings.

The most valuable paintings are owned by museums and are effectively
priceless. In 1962 the Mona Lisa was valued for insurance at $100
million (£336 million in today's money). The Louvre could not afford
the premium so left it uninsured and improved security instead.

It took Leonardo da Vinci 16 years to finish the Mona Lisa. Da
Vinci wrote everything in "mirror writing" – a reflection of ordinary
writing that could only be read by viewing it in a mirror. He said,
"The mind of the painter should be like a mirror".

Picasso said, "I paint objects as I think them, not as I see
them". He also said, "Everything is a miracle. It is a miracle that
one does not dissolve in one's bath like a lump of sugar."

Van Gogh killed himself by shooting himself in the stomach. It
took him three days to die. Mark Rothko killed himself by slicing
into the arteries in his elbow joints rather than his wrists.

London Zoo

WHEN I WAS A KID I used to hear our neighbour Charlie leaving the house at 7:45 am to go to Asda, where he would happily wait outside to guarantee getting some warm fresh bread when the doors were unlocked at 8 am. I never understood the urgency and always said I would never queue for something to open. I thought of Charlie as I found myself waiting alone outside London Zoo thirty minutes before opening time.

Last time I came here I got annoyed cos I paid £14 to get into the place, only to find the sloth asleep at four o'clock in the afternoon. This shouldn't be allowed. If Shamu the killer whale at Disney decided it couldn't be bothered jumping through hoops, they'd get rid of it, so I don't see why this sloth is getting away with just hanging there asleep not lifting a finger. I don't know why it's been given so much space to hang about in – it isn't using any of it. It would be just as happy hanging in a wardrobe.

They say you have to evolve and adapt to survive, yet the sloth does nothing. They say "survival of the fittest", but I think it's "survival of the tastiest". It's a well-known fact that the extinct dodo didn't taste very nice. (Though I bet the last one did. I always find I enjoy my last Rolo or Malteser more than the ones that preceded it. I guess it's just cos I know it's the last one.) I think tasting bad is one of the reasons the dodo died out. It's always the animals we don't eat that become endangered species. Pandas, gorillas, polar bears: all stuff in danger, and all stuff not available at the butcher's. The cow would never die out cos the newspapers would do a big campaign. I can see it now: "Save the Sunday Roast". If polar bears are dying out, we should add them to the meat to eat list. I think we could do with another meat as there doesn't seem to be that much choice. Beef, lamb, chicken or pork. There's seven days in a week yet only four choices of meat, or only three if you're Jewish. They say polar bears are in danger cos the ice is melting. So not only will they die out, they won't even be kept fresh, which means good meat will be going to waste.

Animals that pull their weight will be around for ever. Horses work and get eaten in France; sheep give us wool as well as chops; cows give us milk as well as steak. But the best has got to be the chicken. They give us so much: chicken breast, chicken legs, wings (the fact chickens have wings that they don't even use but that we can eat is evidence that these animals were designed to be eaten), and that's if a chicken gets past being eaten by us when it's an egg. So you have to say the panda is not helping itself by supplying nothing and just sitting about feeling sorry for itself.

The workers in the zoo were giving me odd looks while preparing for opening time as I don't think they see that many 35-year-old men waiting for the zoo to open. It was 9:30 and the place didn't open until 10 am. Opening times are odd things. There doesn't seem to be any system in London when it comes to opening times. I used to pass a sex shop in Soho on the way to work that was open at 8:30 am, ready for any passers-by that needed a butt plug, and yet you might have to wait until 9 am for somewhere that will sell you a pint of milk to open. London is odd like that – some stuff just doesn't make sense. Berwick Street in Soho is a mix of fruit stalls and sex bars, as if they work hand in hand. It's quite a rough street. All the bananas are full of bruises.

I decided to go for a walk around the outside of the zoo cos you can see all the stuff with long necks for free, as they are hard things to hide. I saw a few emus, a camel and a giraffe. By the time I got back round to the gate, the place was open. I seemed to be the only person in there.

This time the sloth wasn't the only thing with its eyes shut. Everything was asleep. I felt like an overnight nurse creeping around a hospital on a midnight check of the wards. A chameleon opened one eye and gave me a dirty look. It reminded me of the look my dad used to give me when he worked nights and I disturbed his sleep by going into the bedroom to nick some of his change off the dressing table.

The sloth that I saw last time I was here was still asleep. In fact it looked like it hadn't moved since my last visit. I read the information. "They live in trees and eat leaves." I guessed this was down to laziness rather than it being their food of choice. I used to eat KFC more often when I lived across the road from a branch, but I ain't had one since I moved. I also found out that sloths are half-blind and half-deaf, they only defecate once a week, and they need to sleep for 15–18 hours a day. I'm starting to wonder if my Aunty Nora is a sloth, she has all the symptoms. She's been bunged up a bit since getting some new teeth, as she's stopped blending her steak and started eating solids again.

I went to see the chimps before the school trips turned up, as kids take over once they arrive and block everyone else's view. On the way I passed some animals that aren't that exciting. Things like tapirs, otters and goats are never gonna attract the crowds. I wondered if the zoo gets one of these animals chucked in for free when it buys a crowd-puller like an elephant or an ape, like a two-for-one offer. I walked past some bearded pigs. I don't know if this is how they've evolved or if the zoo keepers stuck the beards on so the pigs gain more interest. If I see a rhino wearing springy-eye glasses, I'll be suspicious.

The chimps were awake. The older chimp was sat in a pile of straw scratching itself while the kid chimps ran riot, fighting and chucking the straw all over the place. The older one didn't seem that bothered about them messing about – she looked like one of them

BEARDED PIG

single mums you see on the TV programme *Supernanny* who have gone past caring. But then I suppose when defecating in your hand and throwing it is normal, at what point would the older chimp step in and shout at them? It is odd how human they are, though. Someone told me about some monkeys in an Australian zoo who enjoyed smoking fags. Visitors would pass the cigs through the bars already lit, and after a while the monkeys picked up a bit of an addiction. Maybe this is them evolving. For years we've dressed up chimps to look like humans and let them have tea parties, so it was bound to happen as all smokers like a fag after a brew. Some people say it's cruel to keep them locked up, but I thought they looked quite happy. It's the same as how people worry about testing drugs on animals, whereas I think it all depends on the situation: if the drug's aspirin and the chimp has a headache, is it still wrong?

A few more visitors started to appear. An old couple stood out of the crowd. The woman was smartly dressed but was caked in bright make-up that would have given the chameleon a headache. Her lipstick was a luminous pink and went over the edges of her thin lips. I say if you're no good at colouring in, don't wear lipstick.

I don't like lipstick much due to a woman who lived on the estate where I grew up who used to put on loads

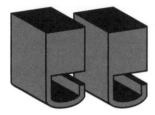

What I've learnt

Bears, before they hibernate, pack their anus with a kind of mud tampon to stop red ants crawling up them and biting and waking them up.

Noel Fielding

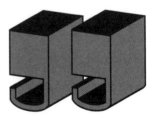

of make-up and lipstick and shave her eyebrows off but then draw them back on. She was that coloured in that she looked more like a cartoon than a real person. She was known as Miss Piggy and would only talk to people via a big mirror that she carried in her handbag. She used to walk round Kwik Save supermarket eating the biscuits without paying for them, but the people who worked there were too scared to say anything. I think she ate all the profits as I've heard that all the Kwik Saves are now closed.

The old woman in the zoo looked like she could have been good-looking when she was younger. Her husband wore a navy blue suit, which was a bit too big for him, complete with tie. I wondered why they'd come here so dressed up. Maybe they came here on their first date many years ago. Then I thought they looked like they might be Italian tourists, as Italians always seem to make an effort to look smart. I followed them into the reptile building. They never spoke. It's odd how people who've been together for years do that. I could understand it if they were in a restaurant, sat quietly enjoying a meal, but here they were looking at a frog that can kill a man and they still had nothing to say to each other. I hope I never get to an age where nothing ever impresses me.

I looked at the lizards. There was one called a shingleback, also nicknamed "the sleepy lizard". I saw these on a BBC programme with David Attenborough. Once they've found a partner, they stick with each other for life. Some have been together for more than 20 years. Though I think they may as well stick with the same partner for life as they all look the same anyway. I left the reptile building. The old couple were sat on a bench. They had similar characteristics to the sleepy lizards. They were eating Cornettos, which confused my idea of them being Italian as I'm not sure Italians would eat a Cornetto, as it seems a bit too predictable. That's the last time I saw them, as the zoo started to get crowded.

I went and had some lunch. The canteen wasn't too busy. There seemed to be more staff working in there than there were customers eating. Mind you, I'm not surprised it wasn't busy: three sausages, beans and chips and a coke came to £10.80p! The saying shouldn't be "too many cooks spoils the broth", it should be "too many cooks puts the prices up". I don't know why they bother putting up signs asking people not to feed the animals – at them prices there's no chance of that happening. I sat and read the guide book that I'd bought while I ate me dinner. Here are some of the facts from it:

The name gorilla comes from the Greek word gorillai, meaning a "tribe of hairy women".

The blue poison dart frogs get their name from a diet of ants and poisonous insects. The poisons they eat enable them to secrete potentially deadly toxins.

Pelicans' feathers weigh more than their bones.

I went to the insect house. I think insects are the most amazingly weird things in the world. There were cockroaches, locusts, spiders and ants, but the thing that impressed me most was the stick insect. The last time I'd seen one of these was at school when some kid brought one in on pets day. The school didn't do one of these days again cos of the havoc that was caused. Kids took in cats and dogs, so they didn't get on; someone took in a ferret, which nipped a pupil; a hamster escaped and wasn't found; and my pet magpie almost ate the stick insect. The stick insect that the lad brought to school wasn't that good at looking like a stick – it looked more like a green toothpick with legs – but the one in the zoo was the spitting image. I was looking in the glass box for about five minutes before I realized it was right in front of me all the time. It's the best camouflage I've ever seen. It was as twig-like as it could possibly be. It stayed perfectly still, to the point where it may as well have been a real twig. The daft thing is, though, I read that their enemies include birds, and birds land on twigs – so why look

This twig is similar to the stick insect I saw.

like one of them? They'd be better off trying to look like a cat. I wondered if stick insects ever think a stick or a twig is another stick insect. A real stick would be the equivalent of a blow-up doll to them.

If reincarnation does exist, I wouldn't want to come back as a stick insect. I'd rather come back as a real twig: at least I wouldn't have any enemies, and I'd be the real thing as opposed to an imitator. Saying that, it could be worse. I've heard the giant swallowtail caterpillar looks like bird poo, which isn't a great look is it.

On pets day we had to stand at the front of class and talk about our pets. The kid with the stick insect struggled to make it sound exciting. He said the best thing about them is they're really cheap to keep, which I thought wasn't the best reason to have one. Bamboo isn't that expensive, but I wouldn't want a panda living in me house. My pet magpie wasn't expensive to feed, but it did pop the tyres on my Raleigh Grifter a few times, so I got rid of it (the magpie, not the Grifter). Me mam kept telling me it wasn't wise to have a magpie as a pet, as if you see one magpie it's supposed to be a sign of bad luck. Saying that, my magpie brought plenty of luck to the fella who owned the bike shop cos tyres for a Raleigh Grifter weren't cheap.

The thing that amazed me most on my trip to the zoo was seeing how things have evolved. A lot of creatures have started lying. They've gone from having great camouflage, to developing poisonous bites, to then letting enemies know they are poisonous by having brightly coloured skin. But now quite a lot of them just have the bright colours to make predators think they are dangerous, when in fact they are lying and are harmless. So I'm guessing that soon the predators will evolve to spot when they are being lied to or cheated, which is something humans have already learnt to

do – which is how, no matter what anyone tells me, I don't believe sausage, beans, chips and a coke should ever cost £10.80p.

ANIMAL FACTS

The world's smallest dog was a Yorkshire terrier owned by Arthur Marples of Blackburn. Called Sylvia, she lived for two years and reached 2.5 inches tall and 4 oz in weight. She died in 1945.

The world's smallest horse is Thumbelina, a 17-inch-tall dwarf miniature horse born in 2001 in St Louis, Missouri. Thumbelina is too small to join a herd of normal horses and instead mingles with small dogs.

The world's largest bird was gigantoraptor, which lived 85 million years ago and grew to 26 feet long and 20 times the weight of a man. It was covered in feathers and had a massive parrot-like beak as big as a man's head.

Some scientists say elephants went through an aquatic stage in evolution and developed trunks for use as snorkels. Even today elephants are sometimes found miles out at sea.

Elephants sleep for only two hours a day. Koalas sleep for 22 hours a day.

The only animals besides human beings that are thought to laugh are chimpanzees, gorillas, dogs, orangutans and rats.

Day at library

IT'S MAD THE AMOUNT of books that have been printed. One author reckons we're getting to the point where there are more people writing books than reading them. I put that down to the fact that most people enjoy talking more than they enjoy listening. I'm one of the few who doesn't. If I had to give up my mouth or my ears, I'd definitely get rid of the mouth. You learn nothing from your own talking. I know everything I'm going to say, I never surprise myself.

I've never been into using the library. I don't like borrowing things as I always worry about damaging or losing them. There was a library at school but I rarely used it as there wasn't that many books in it, and the room was mainly used as somewhere for ill kids to go and sleep. For ages this is why I thought you had to be quiet in a library, so as not to wake up any ill people.

Another reason I don't go to the library is that I don't read that many books. People have asked me what my favourite classic novel is, but I've never read one. The way I see it, there's no rush to read the classics as they'll always be around. I might read one when I'm older. If I do, they'll be even more classic by then.

It was Suzanne's idea that I should join the local library as it would be a place where I could go and sit and work. She knew the building work going on in the block that we live in was annoying me; the heating didn't work properly due to the faulty boiler; plus we didn't have a sofa as we'd sold the old one to some mates before the new one arrived. Eight weeks we had to wait. We were sitting on cushions and it was starting to do our heads in. There's a flat across from ours that we can see into, and it's owned by some Chinese people who always sit on the floor around a low table. I'd thought they did this as part of some old Chinese belief, but now I'm wondering if it's just because they're in the same situation as us and their new sofa also hasn't turned up.

Suzanne thinks I should read more. She says there's nothing better than a good book to get the emotions going, but I don't think any book could get my emotions going that much. The odd book I have read has never made me laugh or cry. I'm not that good at reading, so words on a piece of paper can't get my emotions going. If someone has to give me really bad news, they should write it down rather than telling me as I won't be as shocked or upset. I don't buy that many books either cos we live in a really small flat and don't have the storage space for them. Suzanne keeps buying the odd one and sneaking it into the flat. She brought a big book home by Terence Conran, called *Small Spaces*, which is full of tips on how to make small flats feel bigger. I've told her getting rid of that big book would help. She said it's a good coffee table book that you can look at again and again. The fact we ain't got a coffee table due to lack of space didn't enter her head.

I felt nervous about going into the library. I felt like I was going into somewhere that wasn't really aimed at me. I hung about the entrance for a bit and read the notices.

"Chess & bridge competitions on Thursdays from 6 pm." "Spanish storytelling evening the last Friday of each month." "MPFREE ZONE – NO IPODS." Good one that, I thought. There was a bell you could ring if you needed help in a wheelchair, and a sign that said "NO PETS but blind dogs are welcome". A sign aimed at the blind is something I've never seen before. A library is the last place I'd thought I'd see a blind person. Them, and Tourette's sufferers.

I entered. The decor was all shades of brown. The only other colour came from a few plants. Not nice-looking plants, though: there was a cactus and a few of the ones that have thick, rubbery-looking leaves. Me Aunty Nora has loads of them. She takes a cutting off every plant she passes, she's like Edward bloody Scissorhands. I think these plants are called rubber plants. They're the sort of plants that can survive in the harshest of conditions, but end up in places like libraries and dentist's waiting rooms. Seeing as Nora spends a lot of time in doctor's waiting rooms, this is probably why she has a lot of rubber plants.

It was too quiet for my liking. All I could hear was a buzz from the fluorescent lights and the odd cough. I associate coughs with libraries and snooker matches, as it's the only time I ever notice them. The woman at the counter looked over her glasses (people who read a lot always have glasses, which is enough evidence for me that reading wears your eyes out, even though my English teacher didn't agree with me). She didn't look happy in her work and looked quite old, even though she probably wasn't. I wondered if she was tired and didn't sleep well due to the fact that her ears are in silence all day, so when she goes home and goes to bed there would be more noise than her ears are used to in her working hours. Work can really mess up your body. I had a mate who worked in a toilet in a club doing that thing where they pass you the soap and a towel to dry your hands. He said the main perk of the job was that he could have loads of loo breaks, but his bladder got lazy cos it never had to get used to holding liquid cos he would empty it every ten minutes or so. When he left the job and went on to to be an electrician, it took ages for him to go back to not using the toilet as often.

I got off to a bad start in the library as I wasn't wearing the right clothing. Everything seemed to make a noise. The pockets on my combat pants were so big they let the change rattle about. Not a good design, really – if I was in combat the enemy would have heard me a mile off. And my nylon waterproof coat rubbed as I walked. I was getting looks. The only other noise came from an old fella who kept muttering to himself and breathed quite heavily, but people didn't give him the dirty looks they were giving me. I went to the nearest aisle. It featured books on the art of Japanese swordsmanship. You wouldn't think so much could be said on the topic. I picked one at random: it was a step-by-step guide to sword fighting using stickman-style drawings, which were hard to follow. It looked like the 70s kids' animation *Bod* had been re-done by Quentin Tarantino. I looked to see when it was last stamped out: someone had borrowed it in July 1983. I was eleven when this book last left the library. This is why I don't like Suzanne buying books – they hang around forever even though you're not using them. I have a rule that if something in our flat doesn't get used within three months, it's got to go. Suzanne got annoyed with me in March when she opened the top of the wardrobe to find I'd got rid of the Christmas tree, but a rule is a rule. I wouldn't be that bad if she wasn't such a hoarder.

"Suzanne, these chocolate liqueurs we got as a gift I don't like 'em and you don't like 'em. Why we keeping 'em?"

"Just in case", she says.

The world is clogged up with stuff because of people saying "keep it just in case". The library is keeping this sword-fighting book "just in case" an old Japanese sword-fighter happens to be on holiday in London and needs to be reminded of an old sword-fighting move. The library needs to use my three-month rule.

I read that there are now that many books that there isn't enough time in a person's life to read just the titles alone.

Maybe we have too many books because there are too many words. I thought I'd look in a dictionary to see how many of the words I'd heard of. There was about 20 different dictionaries to choose from in the library. I picked up the *Chambers Concise Dictionary*. I started on the first page, and out of around 40 words I only recognized about six. One of which was aardvark. A word that I've never used, apart from now, and even if I did want to talk about those animals I'd probably say anteater instead. That's a good name as it says what it does. It might not be great for the animal's morale being named after what it eats, but it works. If you found an anteater that was weak and needed food, you'd know exactly what to get it, due to its useful name. But if I found a starving, stranded badger, I wouldn't know what to give it. Saying that, I've only ever seen dead badgers.

Some things get given new names, which is clogging up the dictionary even more. "Muffin" – that's a word that was never needed. Everyone was happy to say "bun" or "cake". I'm sure this word was invented just so Americans didn't feel as bad about eating cake for breakfast. I looked towards the end of the dictionary to see if the words got easier. "Zurf and zarf. An ornamental holder for a hot coffee cup." What's wrong with the word "saucer"? Saucers are another thing that clutters up the house. We got a load of them with

What I've learnt

Aeschylus was a Greek playwright. He was born in 525 BC, and through his plays – *The Oresteia, The Persians* and *Prometheus Bound* – he created, single-handedly, the genre we now know as tragedy. And he died when an eagle dropped a tortoise on his head. Consider that for a second: this man, possessed of perhaps the deepest, most heroic insight of all time – in that split-second we are given between life and death, during which the final mysteries of the universe are revealed to us, he only got time to think: "Wait a minute – was that a fucking tortoise?" This fact represents, therefore, the ultimate triumph of comedy over tragedy.

David Baddiel

our plate set but we never use them. We never used saucers when I was a kid either – they always ended getting used to feed the cat off. We ain't got a cat now so we could get shut of them, but Suzanne won't get rid "just in case" we get a cat in the future.

I had a quick look at a medical dictionary. Some of the words for illnesses are ridiculous. I think this is why doctors' handwriting is always such a mess – the words are that complicated that they can't remember how to spell them, so just put a messy scrawl down. Pneumonoultramicroscopicsilicovolcanoconiosis is a type of lung disease. If someone can't breathe that well, why give the illness a name that they'll struggle saying in one breath? It can only be so that when a doctor says you have it, it makes you think you're in safe, intelligent hands. I suppose if they said, "Ya lungs are buggered" you'd be after a second opinion.

Pneumonoultramicroscopicsilicovolcanoconiosis. That's like the 4x4 car of words. Unnecessarily big and just showing off. If we carry on like this, I think pocket dictionaries will become a thing of the past. Either that or pockets are gonna be massive, one or the other. I wonder if long words came about cos years ago people had more time to sit around chatting and had time to have long words in their sentences, whereas now everyone is too busy. That's why shorthand was invented and abbreviations, due to there not being enough minutes in the day to use all the big words. To this day I don't do joined-up writing. I've never been in that much of a rush. I only use short words so it doesn't take me that long to write a sentence, whereas if you use big words you have to write fast. I also wonder if there are too many words cos there are too many letters. I spent a lot of time in Wales as a kid and was told that the Welsh have less letters in their alphabet. They don't use the letters J, K, Q, Y, V, X or Z, so I don't know what they'd say if they saw a quick brown fox jump over a lazy dog. They just use the letters they do have a lot more. L is a favourite in Wales. Whereas *we* can't use all our letters up, so we go adding them to words where they aren't really needed. Xylophone doesn't need an X, pneumonia doesn't need a P. It's like the word "queue". What's with the u-e-u-e? Whose idea was it to add that when it wasn't needed? We use all these letters cos we don't want any to become extinct. We try to save everything these days: save the pandas, save the polar bears, save the cheerleader, save the letter X. I'm sick of it.

I've always said we've now run out of new inventions cos everything has been invented, but I'm starting to wonder if it's cos we've run of out new names for things. Think of the amount of stuff there is on the world, all of it needing to be called something. That's why you get a lot of doubling up – cars named after animals and people naming their kids after fruits. Even the dot over the letter "i" has a name: it's called a tittle. Why does that even need a name? I remember my English teacher telling us that Eskimos have about 100 words for snow. I told me mam that fact when I got home from school – she said she knew it already and that the reason was so Eskimo weathermen didn't get bored when having to talk about snow every day in their forecasts. I've since found out they ain't got that many words for snow, and that you shouldn't really call them Eskimos cos they don't like it. They now prefer Inuit. But I don't think I'll ever meet one so I don't think it'll be a problem. It would be like worrying that I'm gonna annoy a leprechaun by calling it a gnome.

I nipped down the science section of the library and looked at the *Atlas of the Universe*. It's a book I've seen in a few bookshops and looked at a lot but never wanted to buy, as it's massive. As much as I like looking at space, having a lack of it means I wouldn't want this taking up room in the flat. Plus, I don't think it would be that handy to have as I can't see meself ever being that lost. Might be handy for me mam, though – she's always getting lost. Me mam and dad live in Wales now, and me mam still isn't that good at knowing her way about the place. She has to have their address in her handbag in case she gets lost. She recently bought a tea towel with a map of Anglesey on it from a charity shop. Me dad said, "Yeah it'll be handy, that, if you get lost while doing the washing up."

"The universe is 93 billion light years across", was the opening line of the *Atlas of the Universe*. It went on to explain the Big Bang theory, which I've always questioned. Was the bang really big or did it just sound big cos there was no other noise to drown it out? I must have been standing looking at the pictures for a while, and I got so into it that I didn't hear the old fella who I'd seen earlier come shuffling behind me. "It amazes me more now than it did when I was a child", he said loudly. A few people coughed and rattled their papers as if they'd been waiting for some noise to cue them. He stood there looking at the pictures with me. With the images of space and his heavy breathing, I felt like I was in *Star Wars*. It got awkward as I wanted to turn the page, but he seemed to be reading it. There must be about 3000 books in this library and he decides to start reading the one I've got in my hand.

I started to look at the other books on the shelf while still holding the universe book in my other hand for him to carry on reading. He didn't stop mumbling. I picked

"MORNING CLASS ... IT WAS YOUR HOMEWORK TO FIND OUT HOW YOU GOT YOUR NAME. SO, WHAT'S YOUR NAME?

"MY NAME IS DAISY SIR. MY MUM NAMED ME IT WHEN I WAS SAT IN THE GARDEN AS A BABY AND A DAISY LANDED ON MY HEAD."

"WELL DONE DAISY. WHO'S NEXT?"

"HI SIR. MY NAME IS LILY. MUM NAMED ME LILY AS SHE SAID A LILY LANDED ON MY HEAD WHEN SHE WAS HOLDING ME AS A BABY IN THE GARDEN."

"MY NAME IS ROSE SIR. MY MUM NAMED ME IT WHEN A ROSE PETAL FELL ON MY HEAD WHEN I WAS ALSO PLAYING IN THE GARDEN."

"OKAY ... ERM ... YOU BOY ... AT THE BACK. WHAT'S YOUR NAME?"

"MY NAME'S BREEZEBLOCK SIR."

SIGH ...

"HA HA HAHAHAHAH!!!!!!"

another book, passed the universe book to him, and then moved to another aisle. Whenever I heard his breathing close by, I moved on. It was like playing a real-life game of Pac-Man, moving up and down the aisles to get away. It's amazing that the universe is so, so big and yet I couldn't get away from the heavy-breathing man. I decided to leave.

When I got home I looked on eBay to see if any zarfs/zurfs were for sale, but there wasn't. Instead eBay directed me to some table mats (18 of them for £18) that featured historical places of Britain on them. The counter on the bottom of the screen said that the table mats had been viewed 16 times. Maybe it was other people looking to buy some zarfs/zurfs.

I might buy them "just in case".

FACTS ABOUT BOOKS

An estimated 175 million books have been published. If you read one an hour it would take 19,000 years to read them all.

A million new books are published each year, a fifth of them in the UK, which produces more books than any other country.

Before printing was invented, all books were written out by hand by religious scribes. It wasn't until the 7th century AD that monks first had the idea of putting spaces between words, making the text readable.

Books that have been publicly burned for being Satanic include the Bible, the Koran, the Talmud and the entire series of Harry Potter books by JK Rowling.

According to the Guinness Book of Records, the record for the bestselling book (excluding noncopyright books like the Bible) is the Guinness Book of Records itself. It has sold more than 100 million copies.

The world record for the most books typed backwards is held by Michele Santelia of Italy. He typed 64 books (3.4 million words) backwards without looking at his computer screen.

THE
TUTANKHAMUN
EXHIBITION

admits one

"Probably the saddest thing you'll ever see is a mosquito sucking on a mummy. Forget it, little friend."
Jack Handy

The Tutankhamun exhibition

"WE WILL HAVE ROBOTS doing the housework", "we will travel to work on floating skateboards" and "fishing rods will glow in the dark". That's what the TV programme *Tomorrow's World* predicted in 1983 for the year 2000. They didn't mention anything about building a big tent that would be called the Millennium Dome.

I don't know if you've ever been camping, but normally it's only when you've erected the tent that you realize it wasn't the best place to put it. I think this is what happened with the Millennium Dome. I saw them build it from scratch cos I lived across the other side of the Thames from its plot

– a huge, derelict piece of toxic wasteland surrounded by cement factories, gasworks and freight containers. Other than that it was lovely. Everyone watched as it took them two years to construct. That's another thing with tents: always more difficult to put together when you know other people are watching.

After it appeared, as if by magic over two years, I was looking forward to seeing the inside. We went on a wet Sunday afternoon at the end of January 2000.

It was busy outside. Loads of tourists, and where there are tourists, there are beggars. These were healthier-looking beggars, though. I suppose tourist spots are good areas for begging as there are lots of people with cash to spend, plus foreign tourists probably sometimes don't know how much money they're giving away. This might explain why the homeless man we passed could afford to be sat eating Häagen-Dazs ice cream. As well as the tourists, there were lots of screaming kids all excited about being in the much-talked-about Dome. I felt like a Willy Wonka winner, about to receive an everlasting gobstopper. Instead, I received a heart-stopper: TWENTY QUID a ticket to get in.

We went through one of the 30 or so gates, which led to a big space under the tent containing more tourists and more screaming kids. There were noisy parades, people on stilts and dancers. There was a human body that you could walk through with lots of moving parts. As you walked through it, a sinister voice told you facts like, "Every human starts life as a single cell for 30 minutes" and "Humans make one litre of saliva a day". There was a strange smell in the body. I asked the overly happy tour guide if it was made to smell like the inside of a real body. "No", she said, "it's just the smell of the glue that's holding it altogether. We can't get rid of it".

In every space there was some sort of weird art or dance going on. People were even hanging from the ceiling (though I'm not sure if they were part of the show or paying customers who couldn't take it any more). The problem was, the place was too big so there was loads of tat. It's like when someone buys a big house – they need to buy loads of furniture they don't need just to fill the space, otherwise it ends up looking cold and bare. I've got a mate who's got a big house – I'd say too big, as he's got a dead stuffed owl on a shelf. I ain't got room for a living owl, never mind a dead one. I've heard goldfish grow to the size of their surroundings; so does furniture. You only have to look at pictures of the inside of Buckingham Palace to see what I mean. They have lamp shades the size of Smart cars in there. The way I see it, if you live in a house that you can buy a sofa for without having to worry if it will fit through the front door, your house is too big. Give humans a space and we'll fill it. I'd be happier living in a wigwam.

We finished our trip to the Dome with a few moments in the Chillout Zone, which was a mini-dome where you could sit in darkness and escape from all the noise you'd paid £20 to see. I think it was an area meant for Burger King but the builders hadn't got the electrics done in time.

Visiting the Millennium Dome was like walking round one big, giant poundshop – loads of stuff, none of it useful. We left, saying we'd never return.

Eight years on and the Dome has become a successful music and exhibition venue. Today we're off to see the Tutankhamun show. Suzanne has always wanted to visit Egypt but I've never fancied it as walking on sand wears me out, so I thought I'd take her to see this show instead. A big golden sign above the many entrances read *Tutankhamun and the Golden Age of the Pharaohs*. Under that a smaller sign: *50th Anniversary Tour: The Osmonds. Book NOW.*

I had a dodgy omelette in one of the bars (Suzanne had cold eggy bread) and then the doors to the exhibition were opened. We joined the queue. There was a mixed bag of people – all different ages and sizes. We had a party of five old women behind us who were all excited, not cos they

What I've learnt

That the world is controlled by a network of inter-breeding families seeking to impose a global Orwellian dictatorship through their puppet governments, corporations, banks and media empires. That the world we think is "real" and "solid" is actually an illusion that we decode from frequency fields into holographic (illusory) 3D reality, much like a television decodes frequencies into pictures and a computer decodes electrical and mathematical data into websites on the screen, etc.

The great American comedian and deep thinker Bill Hicks captured it all when he said, as part of a joke, "Matter is merely energy condensed to a slow vibration; we're all one consciousness experiencing itself subjectively; there's no such thing as death, life is only a dream, and we are the imagination of ourselves".

David Icke

were looking forward to the exhibition but cos they'd just spotted Jilly Goolden the wine critic buying a ticket. We paid £22 each plus £4 for the audio commentary device that gives you information on what you're looking at. It was voiced by Omar Sharif. His husky Egyptian voice guided us into the darkened tomb as Egyptian music played. Candlelight flickered to reveal glimpses of Egyptian-style doodles on the walls. It was like being there 3000 years ago – that was until a security man asked me to take me woolly hat off and told me to walk through the metal detector. That never happened to Indiana Jones.

We were then shown a short video that informed us that Tutankhamun's death mask was not included in the show as it's too fragile to transport, but they said they'd made up for it by bringing more "treasures". By "treasures" they meant jugs and vases. Loads and loads of them, and when you've seen one Egyptian jug, you've seen them all. You go from being amazed by the age and detail of the jugs and vases to feeling like you're in the kitchen section at Ikea. Everything had an eagle or a snake drawn on it. If you'd broken a plate or a bit of furniture back in ancient Egypt, it would have been easy to find a replacement to fit with the rest of your collection. All the stuff on show was gear that had been put in the tomb with King Tut. They buried all your belongings with you back then for you to use in the afterlife, which I think is quite a good idea really cos I worry about having to clear out me mam's house when she dies. I don't know what I'm gonna do with all them elves and gnomes she's bought over the years. They had photographs of the inside of the tomb, and all the stuff seemed to be just chucked in. It wasn't carefully stacked or even in any kind of order, they just left it for the Kim & Aggie of the afterlife to sort out.

"Gold ... everywhere the glint of gold", is what Howard Carter said when he first entered the tomb back in 1922. If they did a *Through the Keyhole* type programme on tombs, you'd know from all the gold that this was King Tut's place. Either his or Peter Stringfellow's. Back then, gold was a sign of power. I think Suzanne's mam thinks this is still the case as she always wears as much gold jewellery as she can. Even when she nips out to Tesco's for a loaf, she goes looking like Mr T. from *The A-Team*. Another fact Omar Sharif voiced on the headset was that King Tut was five foot six and a bit goofy. That's something else he had in common with Suzanne's mam.

I read how Tutankhamun died at the age of nineteen from an infected knee. They're guessing he injured it falling off a chariot. Dangerous things, they were. Death traps.

The equivalent of today's quad bike if you ask me. I met the old women again as I was looking at a small coffin made to hold King Tut's liver. All body parts of kings were removed from the body back then and packed neatly into individual small, detailed boxes like some sort of posh Harrods hamper. "That liver is probably in better shape than Jilly Goolden's", said one of the old women, while another was discussing how she's sick of her husband keeping boxes from everything they buy, and another talked about how she'd recycle more if the bins and boxes the council gave you looked as pretty as these boxes. I don't think they were taking any notice of what they were looking at – they'd have been just as happy walking round a car boot sale.

The last thing I read about was the curse of Tutankhamun. There was supposed to be a curse killing off all those who entered the tomb. It was reported that there were 26 deaths caused by the curse, including that of Howard Carter. Even years on in the 70s, when the tomb toured America, a museum security man had a mild stroke that he thinks was caused by the curse. I don't like hearing about things like this as my brain starts playing tricks on me. I started thinking I felt a bit ill. I told Suzanne I thought I'd caught the curse. She told me not to be stupid and that it was probably just the undercooked omelette I had earlier.

EGYPT FACTS

The ancient Egyptians invented paper, the 24-hour day, cement, toothpaste, wigs, leap years and mummification.

The first victim of Tutankhamun's curse was a canary. On the same day that archaeologist Howard Carter opened King Tutankhamun's tomb, his pet canary was swallowed by a cobra.

King Tut began his reign of Egypt at age 9 and died at 18.

Egypt's last Pharoah, Cleopatra, was Greek. Although Greek was her first language, she made an effort to learn Egyptian and so became the first member of her family in their 300-year reign to speak the native language.

Cleopatra entertained herself by testing lethal poisons and venomous animals on condemned prisoners. She discovered that the bite of an asp (a type of snake) was the least excruciating way to die. In 30 BC, after Antony and Cleopatra were defeated by Rome, she committed suicide by means of an asp bite.

Ancient Egyptians were so good at maths that they not only proved Earth is round but calculated its size. In 1250 BC a mathematician called Eratosthenes measured the angles of midsummer shadows in the north and south of Egypt and used the difference between the angles to correctly calculate Earth's circumference.

In ancient Egypt the Nile valley would flood every year, giving farmers several months off work. The pyramids were built by farmers during these off-seasons.

Mummification was popular in Egypt because the dry desert climate tended to preserve bodies naturally. To improve on this natural process, an embalmer removed internal organs from the body, to be dried separately, and packed the cavity with salt collected from desert salt flats. A long hook was used to extract the brain through the nose. The heart was left in place because Egyptians thought it was the centre of intelligence and feeling.

When a powerful or important Egyptian died, his living slaves were entombed with his mummified body.

Cats were sacred in ancient Egypt. When a cat died, the owner shaved his eyebrows as a sign of mourning and had the cat's body mummified. Killing a cat, whether deliberately or by accident, carried the death penalty.

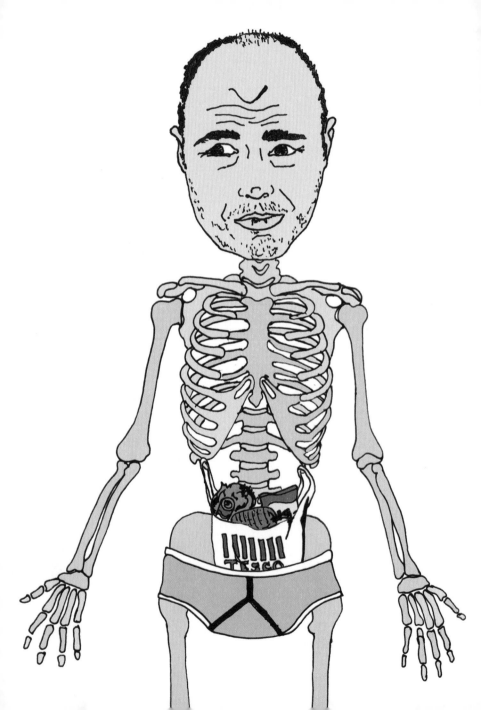

*"Football players,
like prostitutes,
are in the business
of ruining their bodies
for the pleasure
of strangers."*
Merle Kessler

THE

BODIES

EXHIBITION

The Bodies exhibition

IT'S LIKE THE START of the London Marathon. The pace is set by the people at the front, but none of these runners are dressed as rhinos, Postman Pat or firemen raising money for charity. Instead the crowd is made up of businessmen with briefcases, students with rucksacks and women with babies in prams. This was the 200-metre dash from the station concourse to coach A, seat 32 on the 10:36 am Virgin train from London Euston to Manchester Piccadilly, as it's announced that the train is ready to board on platform 14. Even though I'd booked somewhere to sit I still had to join the race as they sometimes don't have time to put reservation cards on the seats. This time they had. Seat 32 was a windowless seat facing backwards in a carriage that didn't have working air con and had a faint smell of sick. As I sat down, an announcement was made to let passengers know there would be no hot drinks served on today's journey, as there was no hot water available. I can't believe this is the same company that in three years time is planning on taking passengers to outer space and back. "London Euston, we have a kettle problem."

Public transport is pretty grim in London. Just a few weeks ago I got caught in the rain with no coat, so jumped into the back of a parked black cab with steamed-up windows to find the driver sat there peeing into a plastic Kia-Ora bottle that he'd sawn in half.

"Give me a minute will you pal", he said.

"Oh sorry", I said, as if I'd just barged into someone in a toilet cubicle that had a broken lock. I should have just walked off, but instead I stood waiting in the rain for him to finish. A few moments later he popped out.

"Sorry guv, I keep forgetting to lock the doors" – which said to me it's obviously something that happens a lot. He then poured the contents of the bottle down a nearby grid. I tipped him at the end of the journey, not for his great service but just cos I didn't want change that had been in his unwashed hands.

On the train I was surrounded by passengers. There

were two salesmen, a kid whose dad was in a different carriage, an old woman with a cough, and a woman who'd stocked up on Pringles and gossip magazines. She started reading them as soon as she sat down. She was in a different zone – she was so into reading the latest gossip on Jordan, Kerry Katona and Paris Hilton that she wasn't even aware of the old woman coughing or the bored kid kicking the back of her chair. I called me Aunty Nora to tell her I was on the train and that if all goes to plan I should get to her house in about two and half hours. I then got out my book on the human body to see what I could learn before going to the Bodies exhibition.

The exhibition was put together by a fella called Gunther von Hagens. He displays "anatomical specimens using a process called plastination". In other words, real dead bodies stripped of their skin and then varnished. He gets away with doing this as he's an anatomist. You can get away with murder if you're in the right job. I heard recently that some scientists somewhere are building a massive machine deep underground that will enable them to recreate the big bang (and yet I get told to turn my stereo down by the neighbours, otherwise I'd get done for noise pollution. Anyway, the exhibition shows the human body broken down and every part cut open for people to see and learn from. All for £10.

I read some body facts from my book:

The human skeleton is made up of 206 bones.

We have more bones when we are born then they fuse together.

A cold brain works better than a warm brain.

There are normally around 100,000 hairs on the head. Blond people have more, with around 130,000, and ginger people have less, at around 90,000. Some would say that's 90,000 too many.

It was hard to concentrate on my book for two reasons, (1) probably being that the air con didn't work – and I'd just read that brains don't work well in heat; and (2) being that one of the salesmen never stopped talking. If he wasn't talking, he was crunching on Maltesers. He was explaining to the junior salesman how he always books the same seat on the train. When the junior asked why, he said, "Simple. Power point for laptop, small personal table, footrest, and bagging area close by so I can keep an eye on my bag". He then had another Malteser. He used the Maltesers like full stops in his sentences.

I decided to look at the pictures in my book that showed the inside of the body, as this took less concentration than reading. There seems to be way too much stuff crammed into the body, which made me wonder how there was enough room in it for the full tube of Pringles that the woman reading gossip magazines had eaten by herself.

I've thought about the body and its layout before. If there's a couple of things I could change, one would be to move the testicles as I'm forever sitting on them. I'd pop them into the earlobes as earlobes don't seem to be doing much, and this would keep the testicles at a nice temperature, which is what the experts say is good for them. And as well as that, having them in the earlobes would make it more acceptable to check them for lumps in public places, say when queuing in a post office or supermarket. It would also put a stop to men having earrings, which is something I've never really thought was right. The other idea is to swap around the heart and brain so that the brain is more protected and not in a place that I keep banging on low door frames. This would also mean cyclists wouldn't have to wear helmets. It would also be good to have a second heart, but since I've seen how crowded it is inside the body, I don't know where I'd put it, so that idea is on hold. Other than that, I think the body is pretty well planned out.

The salesman had eaten all his Maltesers and had moved onto Jaffa Cakes, which meant I could read again as they aren't as noisy. I read that they've managed to stop a cell ageing on a worm. I don't know why they tested it on a

MY EARS

I don't know how to rest my ears
They both sit there listening in
It could be worse
I could have four
Just like a Siamese twin

(Saying that, with four ears there's
no chance of over-sleeping.)

Come on, get up!
It's your turn to
make the tea.

worm, I've never looked at one and thought "that looks old". They always do these scientific tests on the wrong creatures. It's like how when it came to cloning, they went and did a sheep. Why? All sheep look the same so it was hard to see how good the cloning was. I'd be more impressed if they stopped a mayfly from ageing as they only live a day, so they'd be more grateful than a worm. Also, worms are blind, so won't be bothered about how old they look. I'd be interested to see if they can make a tortoise look young. I've always wondered if looking old is the reason for tortoises living for years. Cos they look old, they act old, which means that they move slowly and take more care, whereas if they looked young they might start doing more active stuff and have more accidents and die out.

I was 30 minutes away from Manchester Piccadilly Station. The young kid was bored and was swinging on the chairs in the aisle. I knew we were close to Manchester cos of the smell. There's a McVitie's biscuit factory between Stockport and Manchester that pumps out the smell of biscuits being cooked. Mind you, it was that warm due to lack of air con that it could have just been the greedy salesman sweating Jaffa Cake.

I got to Aunty Nora's gaff. I had a brew while she stood wrapping up individual barm cakes in clear bags and then

Sellotaping them shut to keep them fresh. Everything in her fridge looks gift-wrapped. When you make a sandwich it feels like it's your birthday, the amount of parcels you have to open. I think she's got like this since she heard a lot of bad stuff about that MRSA bug. I told her about the Bodies exhibition and she decided she'd come along but said I'd have to walk slowly cos her knee is playing up. Aunty Nora has always seemed old to me. She's always worn comfy pants, and I never knew her when she had her own teeth. She's had quite a lot of operations over the years so has to take loads of tablets. If you ever buy any pills that say they haven't been tested on animals, the chances are they've been tested on Nora. Her house is like Pac-Man, there's a pill in every corner.

We got a cab to the science museum where the Bodies exhibition was being held. I told the lad on the front desk we were here to see the bodies. I felt like Columbo. We were sent right through the main museum to an empty warehouse out the back, where we had to buy tickets from a bald fella with tattoos in a portakabin, before being sent across a cobbled road to another warehouse. Nora was knackered already, so much so that she had to rest for a while at the entrance by leaning back on one of the warehouse beams. I think a few people might have thought she was one of the exhibits. Once she got some energy back we entered the first room.

The bodies gave off a smell similar to the one you get in the "Land of Leather" sofa shop. There must have been about 15–20 dead, skinned, varnished bodies. All of them had been put into poses that brought them to life. There was one in a playing-badminton pose, another was skateboarding, one was doing some sort of ballet, another was playing basketball, one was kicking a football. I thought sport was meant to be good for you. It didn't do much for this bunch. It was like the stars of *Night of the Living Dead* had brought out a keep fit DVD. What was also weird was that most of these dead bodies were doing stuff I've never done, and I'm alive. I've never played badminton or done ballet.

Around the bodies was a pick-n-mix of body parts. Kidneys, hearts, livers, lungs, a brain and other bits that had been affected by different illnesses. Aunty Nora walked from box to box saying things like "I've had that", "I had a new one of them" and "your cousin had one of them", as if she was flicking through an Argos catalogue. They displayed a lung that had belonged to a heavy smoker and was full of cancer. Next to it was a non-smoker's lung so you could see the difference. It did look a lot healthier, but at the end of the day it was still here in a box for people to look at, so not that healthy.

There was a body that was stood up holding it's own skin like it was holding a dressing gown. This might be the future of dry cleaners. It would be the ultimate skin detox. When you see the skin displayed like this, it makes you realize how, underneath, we're all the same, but some of us are in better-looking packaging. Because they'd all been skinned, there wasn't one dead body that I thought looked better than another. A lot of the time, it's the skin that makes us pick our partners, in the same way as it's the skin that makes me pick which banana I want in a super-market.

I remember reading something ages ago about how they are now able to do full face transplants. I'm not sure if you get to pick from faces that are on offer or if you just have to take whatever comes in. Saying that, even if you picked a good-looking face the chances are it won't look as good as it did on the original owner once it's on your head. It's like when Suzanne picks a hairstyle from a magazine and takes it to the hairdresser's – it never looks as good cos it's all down to the head shape, and Suzanne has quite a square head. I think ideally it would be best to try and do a brain swap so the face can stay on it's own bones. I don't think I'd like it if someone I knew turned up and had a different face. Slight changes are weird enough. I phoned me mam a few months ago when she was full of a cold, and her voice sounded totally different. I didn't like it, to the point that I said it was freaking me out too much and that I'd call her back when her throat was better. So if I turned up and she had a different face, I don't know if I could handle it.

It was hard to tell how old these skinless people at the Bodies exhibition were when they died, as it's the skin that gives away your age. That was the one good thing the Elephant Man had going for him, he could have bought fags and booze under age and yet got away with being an OAP on public transport. He was ageless.

There was a message on the wall thanking the people who made the show possible by donating their bodies. I mentioned in my last book how I once signed a form in hospital to agree to hand over my body bits to anyone who might need them if I die. They said I could sleep on it before making any decisions. (My brain doesn't like sleeping on stuff. The only time it wanted to sleep on something before making a decision was when I was buying a new mattress. I think that's the only occasion when "sleeping on it" could have altered my opinion. Other than that, my brain makes its mind up quite quickly.) I ticked all the boxes, thinking that I'd get looked after better if they thought they'd get to keep my bits once I was dead. I agreed to leave my lungs, heart, liver, kidneys and eyes. But later on I worried about giving my eyes away to any Tom, Dick or Harry. What if the new owner started using my eyes to look at stuff that I wouldn't want to look at? Since then, I've read about cellular memory, which is where a person develops new habits and interests after a transplant. There was a story about a woman who couldn't stand eating yellow biscuits and was rubbish at driving. She thought that's the way it was going to be for the rest of her life, but then, after a heart transplant, she found she was not only fitter and healthier with her new heart, but also really loved eating yellow biscuits and was a better driver, due to the donor having liked yellow biscuits and been good at driving. I reckon more people would be willing to be donors if they were aware of this. It also put me at ease, cos maybe the person who gets my eyes might start to look at things I liked to look at rather than things they like to look at. I just hope I like the look of their wife.

If my body parts are no good to any living person, I'd probably be happy to let the exhibition have my body to put on display, as long as they agreed to pop some underpants on me, cos I noticed even though every organ was on display, people's eyes were still attracted by the knob and bollocks. They never look that great, skin covered or not. I don't know what women see in them.

It's odd to think that people are okay about wandering around looking at dead bodies. You'd never have thought that this would be something people would pay for. I normally can't even watch *Casualty* on the telly cos it can show some pretty gruesome stuff, yet I was quite happy looking at this lot. Maybe that's cos their faces looked quite happy playing badminton and basketball, or maybe it's cos my brain thought of them as waxworks like the sort you see at Madame Tussauds. The weird thing is, this place is cheaper than Madame Tussauds. It's £22 to see a Madonna or a Brad Pitt made of wax, yet you can see a real body with all it's insides for £10. Maybe Gunther will soon be offered bodies from dead celebrities. If people will pay £22 for a wax Paris Hilton, imagine how much the woman on the train who loved her gossip magazines would pay to see her skinless.

Aunty Nora liked her day out with me and gave me a wrapped-up bottle as a gift that I presumed was some sort of whiskey. I opened it on the train to find it was a bottle of Gaviscon.

BODY FACTS

In the time it took you to read this sentence, approximately 30 million of the cells in your body died. Another 20 million or thereabouts died as you read this second sentence. Ten million died as you read this bit.

If all the blood vessels in the human body were laid end to end, they could encircle the Earth 2.5 times.

Every hair on your body comes equipped with a tiny muscle that can make it stand upright.

Hiccuping is a medical mystery and has no known purpose. One theory says hiccups are an evolutionary throwback from our sea-dwelling ancestors that used hiccups to clear their gills. In 2007, a 15-year-old girl in Florida hiccupped for 5 weeks. Charles Osborne of Iowa, USA, hiccupped for 68 years. His hiccupping attack began in 1922 while he was slaughtering a pig and ended in June 1990. He died 11 months later.

If your ring finger is longer than your index finger, you have a male brain. If the ring finger is shorter, you have a female brain.

"Even a fish could stay out of trouble if it would just learn to keep its mouth shut." Anon

London Aquarium

I TRIED TO TAKE A SHORTCUT to the London Aquarium but got lost. I ended up in a part of London I'd never been to before, called St James's. It's a really posh place. I could tell this by the shops – there was a hat shop, yacht shop, tweed jackets shop, briefcase shop and cigar shop. There were no customers in any of them. The most interesting place was an art shop that was crammed full of stuff. Paintings on top of paintings, ornaments on top of stuffed animals, fish in wooden boxes, clocks, soldiers' hats, swords, toby jugs, old doctors' surgery kits, and a human skeleton, who for all I know could have been the last customer who went in to browse and ended up being hit on the head by the stuffed moose head that was lying face-down on the floor. In prime position was a fossil fish with a sign saying it was 58 million years old. If it's been around that long and still no one's bought it, it's clear to me that no one wants it. The shop was like a museum with price tags. I would have gone in to see more, but the owner wasn't there. They'd put a sign on the door with their phone number asking customers to call if they wanted to buy something. I don't know how this shop survives, especially in this posh area. I can't imagine some millionaire who'd just bought a yacht would also be on the lookout for a stuffed toad (which was priced at £27 – I don't know if that's a bargain or not).

It's difficult trying to get directions off people in London cos everyone seems to be a tourist, so they either didn't understand me or just didn't know. I kept walking until I found myself in a familiar part of London. It was Parliament Square, where Brian Haw was still out protesting on the green. He has been there for years, day and night in his tent, with his banners and plaques covered in badges campaigning against war and asking for peace. (Even though he takes the matter seriously he still had room for a humorous badge that said "give peas a chance".) I don't think there's much chance of him getting any peace round this part of London, though, as it's one of the busiest roundabouts in the West End, and on top of all the traffic noise, Big Ben goes off every hour. I found it interesting how Brian was prepared to give his time for free to spread the word about his beliefs, and yet the fella who made money from flogging dead toads couldn't be bothered to turn up to work.

I got to the Aquarium a lot later than planned, which wasn't good as it was crammed with kids on their Easter holiday. I joined the queue. In front of me was a German family of four, who all wore glasses (I can't believe tourists with bad eyes found their way here and yet I struggled), and behind me was an Irish woman with two young kids, one in a pram. I don't know why it was in a pram as it was old enough to keep asking for a McDonald's.

Fifteen minutes later and £14 quid out of pocket, I was in. £14 seemed a bit much. I should have just gone to Selfridges fish counter and asked the fella behind the counter about what he had on offer. I could have learnt just as much about fish from him as they have a massive selection, and I'd get to touch 'em or even eat one. That's the odd thing with fish: we like to look at them and keep them as pets, but we also like

"Two adults please."

to eat them – yet we moan about Koreans who do the same with their pet dogs.

All I got for my £14 was an aquatic guide and a map. A bit late for a map now, I thought. I could have done with that two and a half hours ago. I made my way down the corridor, which had tube-shaped lights either side filled with water that was crammed full of baby jellyfish. They'd used the jellyfish to create a lava-lamp effect. I suppose when you only have so much room, you have to be creative about how you display everything. Maybe they'll have a hammerhead shark squashed into a tool box, I thought.

On the walls were fish facts:

Fish have been on the Earth for more than 450 million years.

Fish were well established long before dinosaurs roamed the Earth.

A starfish doesn't have a brain.

I don't know if the last fact is official or if a fish had got out of a tank when no one was looking and had done some graffiti.

Next was a display that demonstrated how much rubbish, and what sort of rubbish, had been dumped in the River Thames. "At least 1000 tonnes of rubbish is removed from the Thames every year", it said. I'm wondering if this is where the fella with the shop in St James's got his stock from. They'd dredged up old TVs, radios, money, cameras, syringes and stereos from the river. I don't know if we should be taking all this away from the fish – maybe having these domestic appliances around them is how they will learn to evolve into humans again.

Round the next corner was a big tank surrounded by punters. Two fellas in the tank were feeding some fish while explaining that scientists are finding new sea life all the time, and that there is still a way to go before we discover everything that's out there. "We know more about the surface of the Moon than we do about the bottom of the sea", said one of them. I don't know what they are doing working here, then. They should be down at the Science Museum.

They're guessing that there are around 32,000 different species of fish, which makes me wonder why Jesus fed 5000 people with just two fish. He could have given them loads more than that. I think the real reason that sea levels are rising is that there's too many fish in the sea. Jesus didn't use up enough of the fish when he had the chance. If he'd given everyone around five fish, the sea level would have dropped. I think this is why sushi was invented – to get us to eat as many fish as possible in a small amount of time and, in turn, get the sea level down. There was a digital display on the wall in the Aquarium stating that the world eats around two fish every second. It's all down to these sushi bars. The fact they deliver it to customers on a conveyor belt is proof that they can't get rid of the stuff fast enough.

Another thing that makes me think there are way too many fish is the way people struggle to think up names for them and have to reuse the names of animals that are on land. There's a cowfish, dogfish, tiger fish, lionfish, flying fox fish, rabbit fish and elephant-nose fish. They can't keep up with the amount of fish they're finding. I've heard there is also a fish called the upside-down catfish. I'm starting to wonder if this was just a dead catfish that they didn't have time to realise was dead due to all the other new species they were in a hurry to name.

If God did make everything, I wonder if fish were his first attempts at creating life – a kinda trial-and-error approach, which is why there are now so many of them. The deeper you go in the sea, the odder and uglier they get. You can't even guess how old they are, due to their oddness. That's how I judge if something is odd – if I can't put an age to it. There are some really, really odd-looking fish with odd behaviors. It's like God knew they weren't right and tried to drown 'em with a load of water, and the seas are what's left from that day.

FISH ONCE HAD LEGS

To save space in the seas
Nature made fish into amputees

Now sea levels are rising but I won't complain
Cos this gives fish room to grow limbs back again

And I'm really looking forward
To when this time comes

To eating fish legs lightly sprinkled
In golden breadcrumbs

The stonefish was an interesting one. I'd never even heard of these before but they look the spitting image of a stone. The only difference is, these are deadly. It's because of creations like this that I don't like to go into the sea – there's too much danger in it. I used to say I'm not going in the sea due to there being dangerous stuff hiding behind rocks and stones, and now I've found out you can't even trust the rocks and stones. It doesn't seem fair that something that looks so much like a stone can kill a man. Fair enough, if a fella stands on a shark's head and it gets agitated and rips him to bits, he should have been looking where he was going. But to look like a stone and then get upset when someone stands on you seems a bit unreasonable.

There are fish deep, deep down in the oceans that have built-in light systems (this is called bioluminescence) and swim around looking like the MGM Grand in Vegas, but humans don't go that deep so they could turn the lights off, and yet the fish that are dangerous have no sort of hazard lights – they look like rocks or they're see-through like jellyfish and sting you before you've even seen them. I wish they would swap places. And what's really daft is, even though the stonefish's venom can kill us, it doesn't work on its real enemies like sharks and rays as these are immune to it, so it's pretty pointless. That's what I think is daft about the way Chinese learn karate as a self-defence – most of the Chinese population learn karate, so surely it's no longer useful as a defence.

Anyway, stonefish, like I said: bad, bad creation, and God knew this as he tried to cover it up by making it look like a rock. The hairy angler fish is weird too. It's a fish that lives so deep down (around 1000 metres) that not much other stuff lives there, so its stomach expands to allow it to eat things that are bigger than itself as food is hard to come by. I never understand things like this in nature, why doesn't it just move? What's holding it back? It can eat something huge and then not have to worry about eating for a few months. I saw some footage of a snake that also does this. It had eaten a full hippo all by itself. You could see the shape of the hippo inside of it, to the point that it no longer looked like a snake but looked like a hippo wearing a snakeskin body stocking. A bloke tickled it with a stick and it was tickled that much that the excitement made it sick up the full hippo.

I'd hate eating something so big that I wouldn't have to eat again for a few weeks. The most enjoyable parts of my days are the parts when I'm eating. I got really fed up when I was in hospital with kidney stones and was told I wasn't allowed to eat, and that was only for one morning.

Another odd fish I learnt about is the northern cave-fish. It's totally blind due to the fact that it lives in dark caves and has no use for its eyes, so nature just decided to make it blind. I felt like I didn't need my eyes on my holiday to Lanzarote. Every trip I went on involved looking into volcanoes, which were that dark that you couldn't see anything, so what's the point. There is a famous quote that goes, "In the kingdom of the blind, the one-eyed man is king". If there was a kingdom of the blind, Lanzarote is where they should live. They'd be missing nothing. It's an odd saying, though. If I lived in the kingdom of the blind, I'd just tell them I was the one with the working eye. Be hard to be proved wrong. If they didn't fall for that, I'd suggest that a blind man should be king as he'll have our interests at heart, whereas the fella with an eye wouldn't. If I didn't get the king's job I'd be the kingdom's window cleaner. Money for nothing.

I couldn't be doing with being a blind cavefish, though – the sea is not a good place to be if you're blind, not with all them dangerous things in it. The chances of survival are slim. It's the equivalent to being a blind lollipop man. Scary, scary place, the sea. It's mad how people need a licence to drive a car and yet anyone can go into the sea with no knowledge of what dangers are in there.

I carried on with my tour of the Aquarium. I was asked if I would like a picture of me sat on the back of a dolphin, but I turned down the offer. A lot of people were having them done, though. They took your picture on a green background and then superimposed your image to make you look like you're scuba diving or riding a dolphin or sat on top of a whale. This seems to be everyone's dream before they die, to swim with dolphins and whales, yet people are panicking when the news says global warming means that Britain is gonna be underwater by the year 2025. Do they want to swim with dolphins or not?

I turned a corner and there were a load of noisy kids all gathering round a fish tank that had a clownfish in it. This is all because of the film *Finding Nemo*. It's odd how you can have a stonefish that can kill a man, and yet a celebrity fish that does nothing special gets all the attention. All the kids were shouting Nemo's name and having their picture taken with it. It was like watching the fuss around a *Big Brother* winner. I hadn't seen this sort of commotion at an exhibition since some old women got excited at the Tutankhamun show when they saw Jilly Goolden the wine critic in the queue. Even the fat Irish kid who I saw on the way in had got out of his pram to see Nemo. He asked his mam if he could have one. I don't know if he meant he wanted it as a pet or on a sandwich.

I made my way out of the Aquarium (through the gift shop as always) and out onto the South Bank. A fella was selling pictures of the whale that was in the river a few years ago. It was a bottlenose whale that normally swims around the Artic Ocean. It got loads of coverage on the news at the time. Everyone was excited about this creature being in London in the same way that every pupil in my class once got excited when a dog was in the school grounds and the caretaker was sent out to shift it. It was weird as no one really knew what to do about the whale, as it's not an everyday problem we are used to. We can handle hoodies and binge drinkers and terrorist alerts, but a whale? Not the sort of fish you can just flush down the toilet, is it. 24-hour whale shifters are not featured in the Yellow Pages. Men turned up and looked puzzled and a bit awkward as they tried to waft it back downstream, as if shooing away a floating turd in the sea. And as anyone who has been in that situation will know, the more you waft the water, the closer the turd gets. I turn into a turd magnet in that situation. After two days the whale died. According to scientists, the most likely explanation for the incident was that the whale was seeking to return to its normal feeding grounds in the North Atlantic and took a wrong turn, mistakenly swimming west up the Thames rather than taking the longer route around the coast. I can understand how it made this mistake, though, as it is easy to get lost in London.

FACTS ABOUT FISH

* The world's most venomous fish is the stonefish. Its sting is described as the worst pain known to man and can cause victims to ask for the affected limb to be amputated. In Japan stonefish are eaten as sushi.

* A stonefish can survive out of water for 20 hours.

* A lungfish can survive out of water for 3 years.

* A scallop has about 60 eyes, all of them a brilliant blue, but no brain. Sea urchins, jellyfish, sea sponges, oysters, and clams also have no brain and so can be killed and eaten without causing suffering.

* Octopuses have large brains and are among the most intelligent sea creatures. Their brains extend into their arms, each of which can think for itself. Scientists have discovered that octopuses watch each other and learn by observation.

* A giant squid's eyes are as big as basketballs.

* Dolphins sleep with one half of the brain and one eye closed at a time.

* Dolphins are the only animals besides humans that have individual names. Unlike us, they only say their own name, which consists of a special whistle.

*Most brands of lipstick contain herring scales.

WHAT MUSEUM

"The man who reads nothing at all is better educated than

N I LEARN FROM THE

EWS

the man who reads nothing but newspapers." Thomas Jefferson

What can I learn from the news?

"NO NEWS IS GOOD NEWS" is the saying, but when does that ever happen? You can't get away from news these days. It's on the internet, the TV, radio, magazines, sent to your mobile phone, and then there's the free newspapers. Everybody is sat around reading so much news that I don't know how any new news is happening. How much of it do I need to know about? I can't keep up with it, and even if I could, by the time I've read or watched it all, the chances are the news I've read is out of date, so I have to watch, read or listen to more. Are there important things to learn from news, or could I do without most of it?

I decided for this chapter that I would keep a diary of news that grabbed my brain's attention in one week.

Monday
Chinese man gets recognized as shortest adult in the world. His name is Pingping. I've seen the story in a few different newspapers. Some say he's 2 foot 4, some say 2 foot 6. The picture in the newspaper has him wearing a suit that's been specially made for him, but the bow tie he's wearing is of normal size. It makes him look daft. I don't know why he couldn't just go for a casual look for the *Guinness Book of Records* photo. His photo will be next to one of the man with the longest ear-hair and the bloke with the longest toenails, so I don't know why he's bothered getting so dressed up.

I told Suzanne this news and she said, "What are you telling me about that for?" and "It isn't news, it's not useful, you can't do anything with that information". I also read that there's a new record for the tallest horse. It's called Noddy, is 6 foot 9 and hasn't stopped growing yet. I didn't tell Suzanne the news about the horse as I didn't think she'd be interested.

Listened to the radio and heard in the headlines that bored gays are improving maths. I didn't understand this news. It wasn't until they reported the story in full that I found I'd misheard it. It was "board games" that help improve maths. This is another problem with news. Sometimes the story isn't told clearly enough.

More bad war news in the Middle East. I don't know how they can keep this anger up. It's gone on for so long I've forgot how it all started in the first place. The same happened when I watched *Lord of the Rings*.

Called me dad to see if he had any news for me.

"Nothing", he said. "Your mam has been out and bought a new toilet-brush holder, but the brush doesn't fit so she's just using it to put flowers in instead." They waste nothing, me mam and dad.

Tuesday

Woke up to the news that people were happier in the 1960s than they are now. This isn't news, it's obvious, it's probably cos they were younger back then.

It's "Talk Like a Pirate Day" today. I've never heard of it before but apparently it takes place every year. People are asked to dress up like pirates and talk like them. They didn't have time to go into the reasons behind it, but the man on the radio said it makes people in the streets smile. One fella had really got into it by hiring a parrot to have on his shoulder. The report didn't say why pirates used to have parrots. Most pirates had one eye, one leg and a hook for a hand. I don't know why people feared them. If they were around today they'd be registered disabled and would be entitled to so many benefits they wouldn't have to mess about looking for treasure chests. If I only had one eye, there is no way I would risk losing the other by having a parrot with a sharp beak on me shoulder. I learnt nothing from this report.

Bought newspaper from my local shop. No one in there was dressed or talking like a pirate. The news can make things seem bigger than they are, sometimes.

There is talk of environment-friendly funerals. The paper said, "Embalming fluid is made with formaldehyde, which is a carcinogen. Coffins are made from formaldehyde-glued chipboard covered in a thin veneer. Coffin handles are usually made of plastic. These substances pollute during manufacture and after burial. Other expensive coffins are manufactured using exotic and endangered species of wood". Surveys show that more and more people are requesting greener funerals in their wills. I say you're never greener than when you're dead – you're not using up any electric, gas or water, plus you do go green. My dad said he doesn't want me wasting money on a decent funeral for him. He said I can stick him in a bin bag for all he cares.

I must admit, though, it does annoy me how they always bury people in nice quiet areas. I live on a really noisy road and have problems sleeping cos of the racket, and yet the dead get a lovely peaceful park. Why? They could be buried under a motorway for all it matters. Motorways are always being dug up for roadworks so why not shove a few bodies in. Two birds one stone.

More death news. A woman from Peru declared clinically dead woke up as her family prepared to put her body into a coffin. Her name is Felicita Guizabalo Viera. She suffered from cancer and was declared dead by a doctor, but as her family prepared to hold her wake, she opened her eyes. This probably happens a lot due to them being buried in quiet places. Like I said, bury them near motorways and traffic noise will definitely wake them up if they're not dead.

Wednesday
Didn't see any newspapers today as it never stopped raining, so I didn't want to go out for one.

Had some news e-mailed to me from a mate. It was about how scientists may have found a cure for baldness. It doesn't bother me being bald. I'd have the cure if Suzanne wanted me to have hair again, cos I feel like I've conned her as I had hair when she met me. Mind you, her arse is now bigger than when I met her, so I suppose we've both been done.

Another fish has been found with two heads. The report said we shouldn't get worried just cos a few fish have been found with more than one head. The way they reported it made it seem like a major problem. I'm not that worried. It will make them easier to catch cos there's more chance of one of the heads going for the bait. It does make it difficult for them people whose job it is to do a fish census, though. Makes the head count tricky.

Thursday

Me mam called and asked if I was still collecting news. I said yes. She then told me about a bloke who put his whole life's savings into a safety deposit box. When he went back to collect it, it was all gone. Turns out there was some kind of termite in the deposit boxes that loves eating money. I asked if the termite was still sat in the box all fat from the money it had eaten, but she didn't know. I tried to find out more on the internet but ended up reading about slugs. I found out that they are hermaphroditic, which means they are both sexes and can have it away with themselves. I heard ages ago that slugs are causing a major problem with the

What I've learnt

Freud said the sexual self is the essential self – who you are when you're having it off is who you are at your core. So if during sex you say things like "Be a dirty boy for uncle daddy", it means you are essentially a pervert. If you say stuff like "Are you comfy dear? Would you like another pillow?" you are a softie, and if you say stuff like "When the anus dilates and the clitoris is stimulated you can achieve longer, more intense orgasms", you are a sex boffin. My advice is keep mum. As in quiet, not in an Oedipal way.

Russell Brand

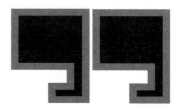

postal service. They've been getting into postboxes as they enjoy eating the glue off the back of stamps, so people have been receiving post and getting charged for postage due to the letters having no stamps on them. Maybe this is why slugs move so slowly and take so long to get anywhere – it's cos they eat glue, so probably sweat glue and get stuck to pavement. The harder they try and move, the more glue sweat they produce, and the more stuck they become.

Friday

Just cos the weather is warm today, more experts are on the TV talking about global warming again. I couldn't hear the full story due to noise from roadworks outside. They are resurfacing the road for about the third time this year. I think this is why the world feels hotter. It's nowt to do with global warming, its just cos the roads and pavements have had layer upon layer upon layer of tarmac on them, so much that we have been lifted closer to the Sun.

We are being warned of another postal strike. I don't know what all the fuss is about. It doesn't bother me as I never get anything nice in the post anyway, it's only ever bills for this and bills for that. They can strike for as long as they want as far as I'm concerned. No post, no bills. I think this is worse news for slugs than it is for me (see Thursday).

NEWS FACTS

The world's first newspapers were made of rock. In ancient Rome under Julius Caesar, government announcements were engraved in stone tablets and posted in public places.

Turks are the world's most prolific newspaper readers, spending an average 74 minutes reading the paper every day. Belgians come second (54 minutes), followed by Finns and Chinese (48 minutes). The Japanese are the greatest newspaper buyers.

Newspaper circulation is falling in the western world because of the rise of the internet, but worldwide newspaper circulation is still rising. In 2008, an average of 532 million people bought a paper each day, compared to only 486 million in 2003.

Some memorable newspaper headlines:

TITANIC: NO LIVES LOST (The Daily News, 1910)

WALL STREET LAYS AN EGG (Variety, Black Monday 1929)

STICKS NIX HICK PIX (Variety, 1935)

HITLER DEAD (News Chronicle, 1945)

THE SPACE DOG LIVES
(Daily Mail, 1957)

HEADLESS TORSO IN TOPLESS
BAR (New York Post, 1983)

GREAT SATAN SITS DOWN
WITH THE AXIS OF EVIL
(The Times, 2007)

The newspaper best known for witty headlines
and puns is The Sun:

GOTCHA! (1982)

STICK IT UP YOUR JUNTA (1982)

I'M ONLY HERE FOR DE BEERS
(2001)

SUPER CALEY GO BALLISTIC
CELTIC ARE ATROCIOUS
(2003)

HOW DO YOU SOLVE A
PROBLEM LIKE KOREA?
(2006)

"Imagination is more important than knowledge." Albert Einstein

Science Museum

"I CAN'T CHANGE A £10 NOTE. You'd be better off going to the underground station and buying an Oyster travel card", said the bus driver. The tourist didn't have a clue what the driver was going on about. Whatever you do these days, you need some kind of card to accompany it. Travel cards, credit cards, debit cards, ID cards, and then there's loyalty cards. The amount of loyalty cards I have is now getting out of hand. These are cards you have to get stamped or zapped each time you buy food, a coffee, petrol, or DIY stuff from B&Q, and then in return gain points to get money off items. I even got one recently for sausages. When I have to get them all out in a shop to find the relevant one, people start gathering round thinking I'm about to do a card trick. I don't know how many of these cards you can have before you no longer remain loyal.

I swiped my Oyster card and went to get a seat while the Spanish man remained baffled by the term "Oyster card". I suppose it is quite confusing. I think the name is from the saying "The World is your Oyster". That's another food I've never eaten, oysters. I'm not a fan of eating any food that is still attached to its house, like snails, clams and mussels. Plus they don't look nice. I think this is why nature put a pearl inside oysters, it was a way to encourage people to buy them – they are like mother nature's scratchcards.

	J.C.Rook & Sons	
1	2	3
4	5	6
7	8	9
Sausages		

Buy any 9 x 1 Lbs (9x454g) and get a Lb (454g) FREE Single or Multiple purchase

There were only a few passengers on the bus. There was a young lad who wore a New York Yankees cap (still don't know why English people wear these caps, you wouldn't get a New Yorker wearing a Charlton Athletic one). He had music blaring out of his phone. There was a couple who were sharing a map of London while gazing out of the window. They got off the bus at Chinatown, which my mate rightly pointed out is not a town, more a novelty street. I wouldn't even say it has enough to call itself a village – it's just a small selection of restaurants, herbal shops and bookies. All the restaurants in Chinatown try to tempt you in by dangling food in their windows, but the problem is, their window display skills aren't the best. They just seem to hang up all their food stock, to the point that you can't see in the place. It's like they use the squids for curtains. Some of the chickens have been hanging there for that long that they have a tan. The Chinese offer some really odd stuff to eat – scorpions, crispy spiders, snake meat and battered bugs. You'd feel daft complaining if there was a fly in your soup. They'd probably charge you and say it's a garnish.

The only other passenger on the bus was a Chelsea pensioner in the seat for the elderly. He had all the usual Chelsea pensioner gear on: the red coat, white gloves, the three cornered hat and all his war medals, which rattled as we hit bumps in the road. He was a cross between a toby jug and a windchime. The rattling would normally have annoyed me, but at least it was blanking out the noise being played on the young lad's phone. The Chelsea pensioner had a Sainbury's bag next to him with some PG Tips tea bags, bread and Rich Tea biscuits in it. The bag ruined the rest of the look. The outfit shows he was a British soldier who'd fought in wars and dodged bombs and bullets for his country, and yet he still had to nip out for tea bags. It would be like seeing James Bond queuing up at a butcher's to buy four lamb chops, it just takes away the specialness of it a bit. You'd have thought there would be a nice bag to go with the rest of the uniform, as soldiers in World War I and II took all sorts with them to get them through the battles – things like pictures of friends and family, tobacco and matches – so a bag would have come in handy. I watched a programme about World War I that told the story about when the war with the Germans paused on Christmas Day and they all had a game of football. The programme was all about how great it was that the very men who'd been trying to kill each other a few hours before could come together like this for a moment of normalness and have a game of football. But what I wanted to know was: who thought it would be a good idea to take a football with them?

He got up off his seat a few stops before the stop he wanted, as his legs weren't as good as they used to be. He got off at Harrods in Knightsbridge. As people got on the bus I watched the Chelsea pensioner get hassled by what seemed to be American tourists wanting a photo. He was moving so slowly, I think they thought he was some sort of pirate mime artist. People stared at his shining medals that informed everyone of his loyalty to this country when once in battle. I don't know if his loyalty gets him any money off at B&Q though.

I got off two stops later and made my way down to the Science Museum. I knew it was gonna be a long day when I found myself in an area dedicated to atoms. A video was playing to no one on a small TV screen. Graphics of atoms bounced about the screen as a voice told you the facts. "You can get 5 million million atoms on the head of a pin", it said. Atoms are dangerous enough – they are what makes the atomic bomb so powerful. So why store them on top of a dangerous sharp object like a pin? They're asking for trouble.

A professor came on screen to explain how he had cut into an atom to find the smallest thing in the world. "It is called A quark." This is what scientists do, they keep breaking things to bits. They are vandals with permission. Also on show was a car cut in half, an engine from a steam train in bits, and an X-ray machine with its casing removed. They all had signs on them saying "DO NOT TOUCH". I don't know why – what more damage could be done? Scientists are allowed to smash things to pieces, yet my warranty doesn't stand if I unscrew the back off me toaster. We're not allowed to learn by taking things apart ourselves anymore.

I had a quick walk through the museum to see what else

SCIENCE

In 1905 Einstein
Came up with $E = mc$ squared

Yet in 2008 British Gas
Still can't get my boiler repaired

Archimedes said "Eureka!"
With no hot water ... I reeka!

caught my eye. There was loads of stuff. There was an area that had all the gadgets that have been invented through the years. Some that seemed good at the time have just faded away. That's the problem with gadgets, you use them a couple of times and then bung them into a draw or cupboard and never see them again. James Bond is a prime example of this, he had loads of gadgets but you never saw him use the same one twice. I bet his cupboards are full of tat.

There was a section about power and how Earth may run out of it if we don't start being more careful with it. I thought this was a bit rich, seeing as I'd just been in a room that had a telly on showing a programme about atoms that no one was watching. "Turn out the stand-by light on your TV" is always the message. I don't know why that light has to be there in the first place. Instead of telling us to turn it off, the makers of TVs should just not fit it to the telly in the first place. It's like the light in a fridge, why was that ever put in there? No other cupboards have lights that come on when you open them, so why does the fridge? It just encourages greedy people to eat at night. If the light wasn't in there, fat people might not notice how much food was in the fridge and would eat less.

It was the "Exploring Space" zone in the museum that was the most interesting. There were bits of rocket engines everywhere. The last time I was in a place like this was when I went to a scrapyard near Old Trafford on the lookout for a wing mirror for my old 1982 Vauxhall Cavalier. I think I would have really been excited about space if I was around at the time the Moon landings were broadcast. The only big occasions I remember being on the telly when I was younger were Princess Diana's wedding and the music video for Michael Jackson's "Thriller". I asked me dad if he watched the Moon landing to see "man go where no man has been before", and he said he slept through it. "They landed too late at night", he said. I know what he means. I've never got into watching boxing on the TV cos the fights always seem to be on at around 3 am. It's hard to get excited about something when you're knackered. I think that's why they ring a bell at the end of each round, it's to wake you up if you've nodded off. Me dad said he isn't interested in going to places where no man has been before. I think this is cos he likes to know what the parking situation is before he goes anywhere.

I read some of the information that was on offer about how President Kennedy started talking about the idea of going to the Moon in 1962:

"I believe that this nation should commit itself to achieving the goal, before this decade is out, of landing a man on the Moon and returning him safely to the Earth."

"Many years ago the great British explorer George Mallory, who was to die on Mount Everest, was asked why did he want to climb it. He said, 'Because it's there'. Well, space is there and we're going to climb it".

I know what George meant. It's like if there are biscuits in our food cupboard, I'll eat them cos I know they are there. If they were not there, I'd have no urge for biscuits. We do a lot of stuff just because it is there. We eat a lot of stuff just cos it is there. I saw some people on holiday eating sea urchins – little spiky-looking things that they hit with a rock to stun and then cut in half. They then scoop out all this black gunk and other parts, just to get to a few small bits that are about the size of a twiglet. It wasn't worth the hassle. They were throwing away more than they ate. It would be like killing a human just to eat their tonsils. I think the sea urchins are still alive while you eat them too. I'm all for fresh food but not that fresh.

Apollo 11 was the first manned mission to land on the Moon, in July 1969. There were three people on board: Neil Armstrong, Eugene "Buzz" Aldrin and Michael Collins. If I'd been in charge of the operation I don't know if I'd have let someone who introduced themself as Eugene "Buzz" Aldrin be part of the job. It's like he's not taking it seriously. Nicknames like that are fine if you fix TVs for a living, or to use when on a CB radio talking to truckers, but is a man named Buzz the sort of man you really want in charge of a rocket? Who were they gonna ask next, the Fonz?

Before today I couldn't have told you who the third member of the mission was. I'd never heard of Michael Collins before. It's a name that doesn't seem like it should be famous. Maybe a middle name like Buzz's would have helped his name sound more interesting. It worked for Eddie "the Eagle" Edwards. Eddie was a ski jumper who had a catchy name and wore funny glasses and is remembered, even though he won nothing at the 1988 Olympics. And yet Michael Collins has been to the Moon and back and his name is unknown. Maybe he should have copied Buzz and gone for something like Michael "Moonman" Collins, or at least gone and wore some funny glasses like Eddie's under his helmet.

They had some problems landing, due to the on-board computers playing up, and were almost forced to land in a large crater with rocks scattered around it (me dad was right about the parking). Armstrong ended up taking manual control of the Lunar Module and parked 12 miles away from where they were aiming to park, but I guess when

What I've learnt

My facts are about lifts.

Otis, the oldest and largest manufacturer of lifts in the world, carries the equivalent of the world's population every five days. Can any other company claim that many people use its products so regularly?

Those 6.6 billion people are also lied to every five days because the door-close button on lifts doesn't actually do anything – it's there to make you think you have control. Does any other company mislead that many people so regularly?

No one has died from the cables snapping and a lift free-falling to the ground since 1945.

And finally, hatches in the ceilings of lifts never open from the inside. Films lie.

Richard Bacon

you've just travelled 238,000 miles you're probably up for a walk.

I read more. It took them 72 hours to get to the Moon. Neil stepped out of the Lunar Module on his own at 22:45 pm EDT (North American Eastern Daylight Time zone) and said the famous words, "That's one small step for [a] man, one giant leap for mankind." It was reported that he messed up his line and left out the word "a", which meant the sentence lost its impact.

I watched a video of Buzz getting out of the module. He got out 15 minutes after Neil as he'd had to stay in the module doing technical stuff like taking readings from dials and meters and turning the stand-by light off. When he did come out, he seemed more nervous than Neil. Even when his feet were on the Moon, he hung on to the stepladder for quite a while before having a wander, a bit like someone at the swimming baths who isn't that good at swimming.

There were lots of photos in the museum. There was a big picture of Neil Armstrong stood on the Moon, or was it Buzz? You can't see their faces in the helmets, and they wore the same suits, so for all I knew it could have been the Stig off *Top Gear*. It definitely wasn't Michael "Moonman" Collins, though, as he never got to walk on the Moon. I can't believe that – he travelled all that way and didn't even get out to stretch his legs. The Lunar Module (the *Eagle*) separated with Neil and Buzz in it, but Moonman Collins stayed in the Command Module (*Columbia*) just going round the Moon like a bank robber whose job it is to keep the car running. In his autobiography, Michael wrote that "This venture has been structured for three men, and I consider my third to be as necessary as either of the other two". That might have been the case, but to me he'll always be like the drummer in the 80s band Bros – he was always at the back while Matt and Luke got all the attention. Whoever it was in the big photo, their pose looked a bit awkward. It's funny how some people just can't relax for a photo. I think it was down to the fact there was nowt to sit or lean on or stand next to on the Moon, and I don't think they had pockets on the spacesuits, so they couldn't even do a hands-in-pockets pose. If it was me having the photo done, I would have got Earth behind me and tried to make it look like I was holding it in my hand, maybe balance it on my head, or both, depending on how much film was left in the camera. Looking at the pictures they did manage to take, it didn't make me want to go and visit the Moon. The fact they took pictures of their footprints in the Moon dust proves to me that there really ain't that much to see up there.

They were on the Moon for 21 hours but only spent two and a half hours having a wander on its surface. I suppose once you've seen one bit of the Moon, you've seen it all. It's said that we know more about the surface of the Moon than we do about the bottom of the sea. This statement makes the human race sound brainy, when in fact it's cos there's nowt on the Moon to know about.

While Neil and Buzz were on their wander, they popped up a flag. It didn't look that impressive, as with there being no wind it just stood stiff like one of Suzanne's mam and dad's towels, which are washed with no conditioner. I hate having a shower at their house as it's like getting dried with sandpaper. Neil and Buzz then went on to collect some dust and a couple of rocks. I've heard that when they were preparing for the lift-off from the lunar surface, they discovered that one of them had broken the ignition switch for the ascent engine. (I bet it was Buzz. I told you he was trouble.) The story goes that they had to start the engines by using part of a pen. This information wasn't in the Science Museum, so it makes you wonder what else they are keeping from us. Was Michael really supposed to keep circling the Moon, or was his seatbelt buckle broke and stuck so he couldn't get out?

238,000 miles, $24 billion dollars and more than 400,000

employees it took to get to the Moon, and all they brought back were some rocks and dust. I bet the atmosphere wasn't good when they unloaded their treasure back at the NASA offices. I imagine it was like it is on the TV show *I'm a Celebrity Get Me Out of Here* when one of the celebs does a task and comes back with only two meals when there are ten people to feed, and everyone pretends they aren't bothered and says things like, "That's great … honestly … don't worry about it … you tried your best". I reckon that's why NASA never sent that team back again.

Eddie "the Eagle" Edwards never ski jumped for his country again either.

SPACE STUFF

If you could drive a car straight upwards it would take less than an hour to reach space at average motorway speed.

Space may be curved, which means that if you travel in a perfectly straight line for long enough you end up back where you started.

Although the Moon looks round from Earth, it is actually egg-shaped, with the pointed end facing Earth.

The Moon is drifting away from Earth by 4 cm a year.

The first person to see the Moon through a telescope was the Italian scientist Galileo. He was amazed to see mountains and chasms on the surface, which people had thought was flat.

Planet Earth gains 3000 tonnes in weight a year due to meteors.

The Planet Uranus was originally named George.

On Venus a day is longer than a year.

"History is merely gossip." Oscar Wilde

Tower of London

MY HISTORY EXAM at school was full of questions based on the Tudor times. The good thing with this was, I could guess at the answers as everyone back in Tudor times seemed to be called either Edward, Henry or Charles if they were fellas, or Catherine and Anne if they were women. By using my gut-feeling method, I got a GCSE grade E. This was my best and only exam result, which proves my gut is brainier than my brain.

On my trip to the Tower of London, I paid my £17 entry fee to then find that the guessing game I did during my history exam would have to continue here today, due to the fact that I couldn't rent an audio guide. You had to hand in some form of ID to get the audio guide, to prevent you running off with the bit of kit. I didn't have any ID on me so had to do the tour without one. I wandered through the different towers but didn't have a clue what had gone on in any of them as I couldn't read the information displays, due to the hundreds of other tourists crowding around them, who must have all come with no ID either.

Thanks to a free map, I did find where Anne Boleyn and Kathryn Howard had their heads cut off. An American man was telling his camp friend that Anne Boleyn was supposed to have been the ugliest of all of Henry VIII's six wives. He went on to say that as well as being ugly, he'd heard that Anne had six fingers on one of her hands. His camp friend said that he hadn't heard that before, but that he's never been up to date with gossip and had only just found out that Oprah Winfrey had six toes on each foot. This was news to me. I was glad I never got an audio guide as I wouldn't have heard about Oprah's feet. The trip wasn't such a waste of time after all. I think as long as you learn something new every day, no matter what it is, the day has not been wasted. Whether it's the names of Henry VIII's six wives or Oprah Winfrey's six toes, a fact is a fact.

I then went to see some royal jewels in the Jewel House. I joined a queue that went on for ages and that, once joined, was difficult to leave due to there being only one way out. I got bored of looking at the jewels as there was just too much of the stuff, and this made me realize why Henry VIII went out with Anne Boleyn. She might have been ugly, but she would've got more use out of all these diamond rings than any other woman, due to her extra finger.

I went and bought a drink, some shortbread and a banana for my lunch, and ate it while watching the ravens that they have knocking about the place. This is when I got told off by a beefeater for giving one of the ravens a chunk of my banana. The saying "You are what you eat" is perfect for beefeaters as their name comes from many years ago when they were paid in beef to guard the Tower. By the size of the fella who told me off, it looked like this was still the case. "It's the job of the raven master to feed the ravens", he said. I think the reason he was annoyed was cos I gave the banana to the ravens instead of him. He's probably sick of beef and would love a bit of banana.

There's an old rumour that if the ravens left the tower, the entire kingdom would fall. There's a lot of superstition when it comes to birds. Me mam told me if you see three swans flying, it means there's going to be a disaster; if a robin flies into your house, it means someone you know will be dying soon; if you see an owl in daylight you'll receive bad news before the end of the day; if you see a bird die in mid-flight, this also brings you bad luck; and yet if one of 'em shits on you, then people say it's good luck.

The beefeater told some younger tourists that some of the ravens in the Tower had been taught to speak and one could bark like a dog. I don't know why we teach birds to speak, there's enough people chatting without them joining in. Bird sounds used to be a relaxing thing to hear, but those relaxing bird sounds are disappearing. There is a bird called a lyrebird that imitates the sounds around it. They can now make the sound of hammering, car alarms and chainsaws cutting down trees. I think we might have a lyrebird living on our roof cos I'm always being woken up by the sound of noisy builders hammering and cutting wood but I'm not seeing any work being done.

"You think we've got a raw deal? I've a mate who's a fire-eater."

After I'd had me drink I left the Tower and went home and thought about what it is that makes people so interested in history. Why are people more interested in the past than they are in the present? Maybe it's cos everything is a bit boring now. I can't imagine in the year 4000 that anyone will be talking about anything that's gone on in my life-time. I think historians will just keep going over old ground about the big bang, Stonehenge, Henry VIII and the Great Fire of London. When someone says the year 1066 to you, the Battle of Hastings comes to mind straightaway, yet if someone says 1980 all I think of is the Rubik's Cube and Garfield the cat. I am really interested in the past, but so much has happened that I feel like I'll never be able to catch up with it all. It's the same reason I've never watched the *Sopranos* – by the time someone told me how good it was, it was on series 4 so I couldn't be bothered. Don't get me wrong, now is a better time to live in terms of wealth and health, but it's just not as interesting to read about or talk about as years gone by. Evidence of this is Samuel Pepys's diary. He lived in a good time to write a diary cos there was always something quite big going on, like the Fire of London or the plague. I've taken a few notes from Sam's diary and taken the same days from the diary I kept, to give you an example of what I mean.

Samuel's Diary: 7th June 1665

This day, I see two or three houses marked with a red cross upon the doors, and "Lord Have Mercy Upon Us" writ there – which was a sad sight to me, being the first of that kind ... that I ever saw. It put me into an ill conception of myself and my smell, so that I was forced to buy some roll-tobacco to smell and chew, which took away the apprehension.

My Diary: 7th June 2006

Woke up to news on the radio that a Russian spaceman who enjoys playing golf has been given the go-ahead to whack a golf ball into space. The ball will go around the world four times before falling to Earth. Hope none of the other spacemen are tenpin bowling fans.

Had chicken wings for tea from Nando's takeaway. A copper was in front of me in the queue. He was using his police radio to take orders from his workmates back at the station. It seems like no one is taking their jobs seriously these days. Police using the emergency radio to order food and spacemen hitting golf balls. What's goin' on?

Samuel's Diary: 22nd August 1665

I went on a walk to Greenwich, on my way seeing a coffin

with a dead body in it, dead of plague. It lay in an open yard ... It was carried there last night, and the parish has not told anybody to bury it. This disease makes us more cruel to one another than we are to dogs.

My Diary: 22nd August 2006

There has been a nude run going on in the Netherlands. The radio did some commentary from it. It sounded like there were hundreds of spectators clapping, then I thought it may have just been the noise of the men's bollocks slapping their legs. I wouldn't be happy doing that. I definitely wouldn't want to win the race cos then I'd probably have a picture of me in the paper coming over the finishing line. Hardly something you'd want to show people, is it.

Dropped toaster today. Instead of letting it hit the floor I stuck by foot out and it landed on my little toe. The nail has gone all blue and looks like it could fall off. I don't think we need nails on our toes anymore. Since the invention of shoes they don't have any purpose. They are more trouble than they are worth.

Samuel's Diary: 2nd September 1666

Some of our maids sitting up late last night to get things ready against our feast today. Jane called up about three in the morning, to tell us of a great fire they saw in the City. So I rose, and slipped on my night-gown and went to her window, and thought it to be on the back side of Mark Lane at the farthest; but, being unused to such fires as followed, I thought it far enough off, and so went to bed again, and to sleep ... By and by Jane comes and tells me that she hears that above 300 houses have been burned down tonight by the fire we saw, and that it is now burning down all Fish Street, by London Bridge. So I made myself ready presently, and walked to the Tower; and there got up upon one of the high places ... and there I did see the houses at the end of the bridge all on fire, and an infinite great fire on this and the other side ... of the bridge ... So down [I went], with my heart full of trouble, to the Lieutenant of the Tower, who tells me that it began this morning in the King's baker's house in Pudding Lane, and that it hath burned St. Magnus's Church and most part of Fish Street already. So I rode down to the waterside ... and there saw a lamentable fire ... Everybody endeavouring to remove their goods, and flinging into the river or bringing them into lighters that lay off; poor people staying in their houses as long as till the very fire touched them, and then running into boats, or clambering from one pair of stairs by the waterside to another. And among other things, the poor pigeons, I perceive, were loth to leave their houses, but hovered about the windows and balconies, till they some of them burned their wings and fell down.

My Diary: 2nd September 2006

Midsomer Murders was on the telly this afternoon so I let Suzanne watch it cos she isn't too well at the moment. I sat by the window and watched the world go by. The Chinese family across the road were cleaning their windows. They are minging. (That isn't the name of the Chinese family – "minging" is a northern word that doesn't get used down south. It means filthy.) It's only a small flat but about five people live in it, plus they've recently bought one of them small Chihuahua dogs. I think they look ridiculous. If it wasn't for humans taking care of them, I'm sure Chihuahuas would be extinct by now. Me mam's mate had one, and she was sat eating a pasty on a wall in Cornwall with the Chihuahua in her lap when a seagull came down and grabbed her Chihuahua and carried it out to sea. She never saw it again. It wouldn't have happened if she'd had a Border collie.

Maybe in years to come people will learn just as much from my diary as we've learnt from Samuel's, as age tends to make things more interesting doesn't it. Leave something lying about for five minutes and you'll always get a jobs-worth who says, "It's a mess get it cleared up it's dangerous. Someone could trip on that!" But if it's left, after a while it becomes history. I wouldn't be surprised if this was the case with Stonehenge. I bet people who lived around Stone-henge when the stones where first put there hated them and complained about the structure that was about to be built – so much so that building work was stopped and the stones were left as they were on the last day of work, just lying all over the place. People are always asking who built Stone-henge, but let's face it: it's such a bad job, if it was my build-ing company that had knocked them up I think I'd also keep my mouth shut. But now, cos they've been around for so long, we leave them alone. I think they're still worried about someone tripping on them, though, as they've put a

barrier around them. Druids are the only ones who get to go over the rope barrier as they use the stone circle as a kind of church. I like the druids. I'm forever being asked to give money to our local church for the upkeep of the roof, but I've never been approached by a druid for money to get them a roof and yet Stonehenge could really do with one. But like I say, it's the fact it's been around for so long that makes us think we may as well keep it. This happened with a road in Manchester on the Mancunian Way (A57). There's a sliproad that just ends in midair cos they found it would have sent traffic to the wrong place, so they've just left it and put some cones up. In millions of years time, new life-forms will be baffled by this road and will probably end up thinking it was a runway for cars that could fly.

I also think it's harder to get something in the history books these days, because there's now been so much history that there will always be something a bit more impressive that occurred on the same date in the past. An example of history getting in the way is people whose birthday is on December 25th. They never seem happy about it. There's no point trying to do something special on your birthday if you were born on December 25th as it will always be better known for the birth of baby Jesus. Another example is the way me mam and dad's birthday is on the same day.

They are never happy that I get them one card between them both.

There's now so much history that people cram it in wherever they can to help us remember it: blue plaques on buildings to let us know who lived there; roads named after people from the past; statues and memorials. Only the other day I noticed the picture of an old woman on the five pound note. She's called Elizabeth Fry. She helped found the Association for the Improvement of the Female Prisoners in Newgate. I'd never heard of her before.

People love the idea of getting in the history books, and this is why the *Guinness Book of Records* gets madder every year. The book of records was set up by a fella called Sir Hugh Beaver, who was managing director of the Guinness brewery. He got into an argument with a mate about which was the fastest gamebird in Europe. He couldn't get an answer off anyone so decided to put together a book that could answer such questions. It was first published in 1954. In the space of just over 50 years it's gone from covering the fastest bird in Europe to covering a man who can pull a truck with his penis. There's no need for anyone to do that (not with the AA or RAC membership being so cheap). People do this stuff just so they can be remembered and get their name in the history books, which is now harder than ever.

Maybe this is why we're trying to find another planet that we can live on. If we move to a new planet, kids in school won't need to be taught about things that happened on Earth as none of it would be relevant anymore. Maybe the history books would be scrapped and we'd start again, leaving out the kings and queens of yesteryear and starting with today's kings and queens of entertainment. Maybe the fact about Oprah Winfrey and her six toes that I heard from the camp American man at the Tower of London could make it in. Not so much history, more his toe story.

FAMOUS PRISONERS OF THE TOWER

<u>1536</u> Anne Boleyn, Henry VIII's second wife. Beheaded by French method of sword rather than axe.

<u>1542</u> Catherine Howard, Henry VIII's 5th wife. Beheaded away from public gaze on Tower Green.

<u>1605</u> Guy Fawkes. Sentenced to be hanged, drawn and quartered after confessing his part in Gunpowder Plot to blow up Parliament. Fortunately for Fawkes, he leapt off gallows in noose and broke his neck.

<u>1592, 1603 & 1618</u> Sir Walter Raleigh, explorer, imprisoned three times. First brief spell was punishment from Queen Elizabeth I for secretly marrying her lady-in-waiting. Second was when King James I accused him of treason and imprisoned him for 13 years. Raleigh occupied himself by writing a bestseller about the history of the world. After release he commanded an expedition to South America to find gold. Failed and was thrown in Tower on his return, before being beheaded in front of the Houses of Parliament.

<u>1679</u> Samuel Pepys, diarist. Imprisoned for incompetence in his job at the Admiralty.

<u>1941</u> Josef Jakobs, spy. Executed by firing squad (last execution at the Tower).

<u>1942</u> Rudolf Hess, Deputy to Adolf Hitler. Imprisoned after capture in Scotland.

TIME
TO
THINK

William Penn
"Time is what we want most, but what we use worst."

Time to think

"TIME COULD HAVE BEEN invented a bit better", I thought to myself while lying on my sun lounger in Menorca. I was going to tell Suzanne my thought, but she was reading her holiday book. She likes to pass time on holiday by reading, whereas I prefer to just sit and think about things instead. Thinking is underrated. I don't think thinking is a popular pastime these days due to the fact there's always something else on offer that you could be doing instead. Maybe people also don't like to do it as much as it's now harder due to noise. My thinking kept getting interrupted by the noisy Spanish builders across the road; the small tourist train that goes past every 20 minutes ringing its bell; the family in the villa next door whose kids keep listening to the same song by Mika over and over again; the music from the bar; and on top of all that was the racket of bottles smashing as they were being collected from the recycle bins, which was so noisy it was like being at *Stomp* the Musical.

I think it is noisier abroad due to the fact that everyone does everything outside. I notice the sound of the birds more abroad. I used to think this was cos there were more birds abroad than there are in Britain, but now I don't think that has anything to do with it. It's just that they have evolved to be louder so their tweets can be heard by each other over everybody else's racket. Foreign people always seem to talk louder too. This is probably why foreign birds such as parrots and cockatiels learn to speak. If we were outside all day yelling at each other as the foreigners do, I think our sparrows would have learnt to chat in English by now.

Anyway, the invention of time. I wonder if it could have been designed better. People are always saying, "Oh there just aren't enough hours in the day", but I say it all depends on where you are. Here in Menorca, the fact that the holiday rep asked if we'd like to go on the all-day trip to a leather factory tells me there are too many hours in a day here. Even if there were more hours in the day, I think it would probably just make people lazy. I doubt any more

What I've learnt

It amazed me to learn that Einstein's theory of relativity has a lot to do with your car's satnav system. According to Albert's 100-year-old theory of relativity, time runs slower when something is moving faster. Don't question it now, just accept it. GPS satellites need accurate clocks to do their job properly, but because they are whizzing round Earth at high speed, their clocks run a tiny bit on the slow side. Fortunately, it's quite easy to set up a bit of software to keep the Earth clock and the satellite clock in perfect unison.

But why should you need to? Well, if the two clocks are out by a millionth of a second, then your satnav will be 30 cm out. If their times are out by one ten thousandth of a second – not a lot really – then your satnav will be 30 metres out, and you, matey, will be driving down the wrong side of the motorway. Oops!

Johnny Ball

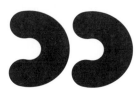

work would actually get done – people would just work a lot slower. I don't know anyone who does anything useful with the extra hour when the clocks go back in summer. They normally just have a longer sleep.

The more time people have, the more time there is to mess about. London won the Olympics in 2006 and yet the event isn't on until 2012. Six years to get something ready is way too much. This means you get people coming up with more and more ideas and spending more and more money, and you can bet your life that the builders will still be running round as fast as some of the Olympic athletes on the day before the opening ceremony trying to finish stuff, even though they've had years to complete it. Six years and a cost of £9 billion to arrange the Olympics seems mad when you think that the athletes themselves are getting faster. If I was in charge, after spending £9 billion on the various stadiums and arenas I'd ask the 100 metre runners to slow down so I got my money's worth out of the track. I can't get excited about that race. Any race that takes less time to get to the finish line than it does for its runners to tie their laces isn't worthwhile. I prefer the slower sports like snooker. Me mam hates snooker and thinks it could be over a lot quicker if they got rid of the bloke who keeps taking the balls out the pockets and putting them back on the table.

I think people have more time to themselves than ever before. It rains a lot in Menorca, so I found meself watching some satellite channel that was showing the old Christmas film *Scrooge*, which featured Bob Cratchit (Scrooge's employee) only getting one day off for Christmas. Now people get loads of time off throughout the year: bank holidays, Pancake Tuesday, Easter, summer holidays – so much time that they don't know what to do with it. So we end up doing things just to kill time, like walking round a leather factory. Good Friday was when Jesus got put on the cross, but that would never happen now cos they'd charge double time, plus you wouldn't be able to get hold of nails as the hardware shop would be shut. When we told the rep that we weren't interested in going on the trip to the leather factory, she didn't give up (I think she must be on commission from ticket sales). "Do you like cheese", she asked, "what about a trip to the cheese factory?" She said it as if the two go hand in hand. I didn't dare tell her I like bacon, she'd have us down the local abattoir. She left us her phone number just in case we changed our minds.

Time was a good invention, but I wonder how different things might have been if we'd come up with it earlier. Would it have made us more advanced than we currently are? If we'd had days and weeks and hours and minutes in place earlier, maybe the fella who made the wheel would have completed it even quicker, as his mate would have been saying, "Will you hurry up with that wheel, you've been messing about with it for weeks!" But then again, it could have gone the other way – once time had been invented he might have given up and said, "I'm wasting me time 'ere … think I'll have a go at fire".

I watched a programme about the Pirahã tribe of the Amazon and how they don't have any system for time. It said they don't bother knowing about colours either, as it isn't important to them. Also they communicate using nothing but whistles. The window cleaner on our estate was like that. Apparently it came about after working on his own for years and not having to talk. The story goes that he fell off his ladder, broke his front teeth and couldn't whistle any more, so he didn't enjoy the job as much and quit cleaning windows. I couldn't understand the problem cos birds don't have teeth but can whistle. Apart from the humming bird. I don't know why the window cleaner didn't try humming.

The other interesting thing about the Amazon tribe was that when it came to numbers, they only counted to three as they didn't need any more than that in their lives. I'm

CAVEMEN

"Cavemen were stupid" is what some say
But they created the wheel and fire

I've just paid 49 pounds for heating this month
And 38 quid for a new tyre!

Who's stupid again?

guessing playing hide-and-seek with them wasn't much fun, though.

I suppose that years ago there wasn't as much to do with your time, as there weren't as many hobbies and pastimes, so 24 hours in a day probably seemed like plenty. But then as time went on, we created more and more things to do, and instead of just creating more time, we tried to speed everything up to fit into the time we had. This is when we invented fast food, Velcro straps on shoes instead of laces, instant coffee, Pot Noodles, Cup-a-Soups and microwave ovens. People even put go-faster stripes on their cars.

I think we've slowed down quite a bit now, though. Instant coffee isn't half as popular as it was in the 80s – people now prefer to faff about with mochas and cappuccinos. Gardening programmes tell you to grow your own veg instead of buying it. Cooking programmes tell you to eat faffy things like sea urchins and pomegranates, and tell you to bake your own bread, marinade stuff and cook lamb for six hours to get a better flavour. I read that some people are eating ostrich eggs – an hour and a half it takes to boil one of them!

I thought we're meant to be living in an energy-saving period, yet here we are boiling eggs and cooking lamb for hours on end.

I think this is going too far the other way. I couldn't be bothered faffing about with a meal I wouldn't be able to eat for six hours – I cook food when I'm hungry. I don't mind waiting 25 minutes for some oven chips, but six hours for a joint of lamb? By the time it was ready I might not fancy it any more. I don't think a meal or snack should take more than double the time to make as it takes to eat. This is why I'm not a fan of oranges. The taste of an orange isn't good enough to compensate for the hassle of peeling it. Some people are worse than me, though. I saw a bag with a sliced-up apple in it in my local supermarket. How much of a hectic life must you have if you ain't got time to cut an apple?

I think this is why scientists want to create a time machine. It would allow us to take our time with things like cooking lamb for six hours, but then we could also gain the time back. But I don't like the idea of it. Look at the trouble Doctor Who gets into with it. I also think people would abuse it. People are already too careless. If they knew they could just go back in time and put things right, they'd be even more careless. Cher sang the song "If I Could Turn Back Time" about how she wished she could turn back time just so she could stop an argument that she'd had. If this is the sort of stupid thing people would be doing with time travel, I don't think we should encourage it.

So, time and the calendar. We have 12 months a year, 365 days, seven days a week, 24 hours a day, 60 minutes to an hour, 60 seconds to a minute. All man-made, and it's never been changed. It's odd to think that at the beginning of time there was no proper time system other than day and night. It's like the invention of the mobile phone – we managed without it for ages, but now that it's here it's hard to imagine life without it. But while mobile phones have been improved and now feature cameras, video recorders, e-mail and music players on them, time has remained the same. So I wonder if it's about time that we changed time. I decided I'd act as an inventor and give some thought to how a new time system would work best.

I like to think of ways of changing things for the better, and I've had a few good ideas over the years. One being a clippable mat. It clips to the bottom of your cup or mug and saves you having to use saucers or having to worry about where you can put your hot drink. Most people I've told think this is a good idea. Me mam said she'd buy a couple, but me dad said she isn't a great guide as to whether or not something is needed, as she buys all sorts of tat. Recent items being the gnome that whistles as you walk past it and a silent wind chime for people who like the garden ornament but can do without the noise. It's odd how some things catch on and others don't. I saw a tie with pockets, which I thought was a saleable design. I've never understood the purpose of the tie, and I thought this idea gave it one. Scarves are okay and have a job to do. Pants, vests, hats, socks and shoes all make sense to me. Braces are a bit odd but at least they do something. But ties – I don't know how they ever caught on. It's the "garnish" of clothing. So I thought the tie-with-pockets idea would fly off the shelves. There were various-sized pockets on the back of it: places for credit cards, spare change, keys and shopping lists. I don't like to use a bag as they are easy to put down and forget, whereas a tie never leaves your neck. For people who carry a lot of stuff, I thought the same idea could be adapted for scarves. As it happens, no one cared for the idea and I've never seen anyone wearing one. Weird innit.

So, time, which way should I change it? People always seem to be busy and complaining there isn't enough time or saying "In a minute!" whenever asked to do something, but I think we've got more free time in this country than ever before. Evidence of this is how songs are now a lot longer than they used to be. In the 50s and 60s, songs used to only be around two minutes long, but now on average they're around four minutes, which proves people have more free time. Then there's the "all-day breakfast" we've started being offered, which I think doesn't help progress – it just encourages people to sleep in. I went on holiday to the Canary Islands and if you weren't up and in the canteen for breakfast by 9 am, you didn't get any. Maybe that's why they have siestas over there.

So, here's my proposal. I'm thinking that years are too long – 365 days should be taken down to about 200. This will cheer people up as birthdays and Christmases will come around sooner. It will also have the knock-on effect of making people live longer. News will become older quicker, and seeing as time is a great healer, things will be healed quicker. Kids will also age quicker, which will make them mature quicker. The change means there will be fewer months – only six to a year, starting with December (I'll have to keep Jesus's birthday as you can't mess with religion or it would cause a riot) and ending with May (keeping Easter, so fat people and kids are still happy). I'm not too worried about the seasons, as since global warming began, the weather seems to do what it wants anyway. Each month will have 4 weeks, and I'd add an extra day to the week so that people work six and are off for two. This would increase productivity, making up for the lost days in the shorter year, but people shouldn't moan as their holidays will come around sooner. Criminals will be put off crime, as what was a 10-year sentence would now become an 18-year sentence, which, even though it's the same length of time, would seem longer mentally. This would work the same way with ill people: when the doctor tell's them they only have two years to live, the new system would mean they have over four years, which I think would cheer them up.

I think I'll end it there, not cos I'm out of time but because of another thing that controls our life. The weather. It's started raining again.

"The rain, in Spain, stays mainly, in Spain."

I wonder what time the leather factory closes?

What I've learnt

Karl always asks impossible questions and expects me to know the answers. He'll go to bed asking about "planets 'n' that" and wake me up wanting to chat about the workings of the immune system. He likes to tell me stuff, stupid facts usually, so that I'll remember them for him. He thinks his brain runs him, so he'll never be able to store and recall this useless information. He wants my brain to do that for him.

Asking "What's the best thing you've learnt?" is typical of Karl. It's like he thinks people spend all their time just contemplating how great insects are or how some bloke once grew a finger back using "pig dust". I've told him I can't think of one defining thing – having spent seven years in higher education, my brain's not full of trivia or facts, maybe it's full of practical stuff for my job. I have learnt one thing over the last 14 years with Karl, though: he manages to out-stupid himself all the time. Even if you think you've heard the daftest thing ever come out of his mouth, he's always able to top it. He makes me laugh every day, though, so I can't complain.

Suzanne (Karl's girlfriend) X

I'd like to say thanks to the following people who supplied me with stuff to fill this book with: Ricky Gervais, Russell Brand, Johnny Ball, Noel Fielding, Danny Wallace, Richard Bacon, David Baddiel, David Shrigley, David Icke. Thanks also to Jess Bentall for book design and artwork for chapter openers and to Ben Morgan for additional facts.

Alright